T0248375

"*Jump on the Train* brings me back to the 70s. Style design touches most of Jerry's ventures, which I think is why he did so many different things after leaving fashion. His story reads more like fiction than fact."

**Elie Tahari,** FASHION DESIGNER

"*Jump on the Train* is a fast and furious read, like a roller coaster ride that takes you through the excitement and downfalls of the New York scene from a quintessential New Yorker. And I thought my life was complex."

**Domingo Zapata,** ARTIST

"*Jump on the Train* is a must-read for serial entrepreneurs, real estate enthusiasts, and anyone captivated by the fast-paced world of business and entertainment in New York City. Whether you're looking for inspiration, practical insights, or simply a thrilling narrative set against the vibrant backdrop of the Big Apple, Jerry Rosengarten delivers."

**Shane Neman,** AUTHOR, *NIGHTLIFE LESSONS*

"I appreciate all the courtroom drama in Jerry's legal battles. They're fascinating to read and show the complexity of real estate and property law. Even if you're not a lawyer, you won't be able to put this book down."

**Marty Bockstein,** ATTORNEY (RETIRED)

"The author's life trajectory can be characterized by meager childhood educational opportunities, steady resolve facing adversity, and the opportunities stemming from bouts of creative hypomania. That energy has been eventually harnessed by a woman, his wife, to his and our great benefit as the description of his journey should be an inspiration to anyone regardless of their start in life."

**Francis Mas, MD,** PSYCHIATRIST

"I've built some beautiful projects over a long career, and I give Jerry Rosengarten credit for the real estate he's developed. The escapades in *Jump on the Train* are mostly new to me and fun to read; I wish I were there."

**Daniel Lebensohn,** REAL ESTATE INVESTOR/DEVELOPER

"From his seat on a bullet train that hurtles over time, Gerald Rosengarten guides us through the various chapters of an eclectic, well-lived life. Undaunted by a severe learning disability and lacking a college degree, Rosengarten's story is poignant yet gritty but ultimately inspiring and triumphant. *Jump on the Train* has a subtext: 'stop your kvetching and pull up your boots.' This is a true 'hero's journey,' the story of an entrepreneur from a bygone age, and its lessons are needed now more than ever."

**Peter J. Fox,** SCREENWRITER

To my brother, Howard . . .
Through it all, you will always be my longest love.

www.amplifypublishing.com

*Jump on the Train: A Dyslexic Entrepreneur's 50-Year Ride from the Leisure Suit to The Bowery Hotel and a New York Solar Farm . . .*

For more information, please contact:
Amplify Publishing, an imprint of Amplify Publishing Group
620 Herndon Parkway, Suite 220
Herndon, VA 20170
info@amplifypublishing.com

Library of Congress Control Number: 2023910561

CPSIA Code: PRV1023A
ISBN-13: 978-1-63755-616-0

Printed in the United States

# JUMP
## on the
# TRAIN

A DYSLEXIC
ENTREPRENEUR'S
50-YEAR RIDE FROM
THE LEISURE SUIT
TO THE BOWERY HOTEL
AND A NEW YORK
SOLAR FARM...

**Gerald Rosengarten**

# Contents

# Introduction
## 'Get on the Train or Let It Go By'

When you live in New York City, you invariably hear an old saying; "You either get on the train or let it go by." This urban adage not only applied to my daily commute, but it has been the metaphor of my career. I have never been able to hold a job working for someone else for very long, and I often worked several jobs at the same time. I often have found myself jumping from one subway line to another, heading in many different directions.

Decisions weren't often based on deep insights. On the contrary, I usually knew nothing about the things I was going after or how I would get there. An opportunity simply needed to be appealing to me, and I was ready to jump onboard. There was nothing to lose. I had no money, no college degree, and no mentor with a bright light to guide me. I was on my own, moving at high speed. On top of this, I was dyslexic (as I learned many years later) and couldn't read for beans.

I enjoyed inventing change—something I learned was my best strategy for working with my dyslexia. From starting fashion crazes in the wild and loose 70s and helping to legalize artists' lifestyle loft living to developing the popular Bowery Hotel that is frequented by celebrities today, it's been a wild New York City ride.

Now, as I seek to create other challenges in my later years, my passion directs me toward protecting the environment for the sake of my grandchildren and future generations. I'm proud to have built one of the largest solar farms in the Northeast region and exposed the hypocrisy of our government and the utilities. But none of this came without obstacles, heartaches, and lawsuits. My attorney, Lou, never failed to remind me, "Do you remember what a nightmare that was?" And so it continues.

This journey begins with my childhood to give you an understanding of what shaped me early on. The chapters that follow are each a snapshot of a period of my life and career. The stories in this book reflect my perception and memory of events that happened many years ago. Some names and titles have been changed. The rest is shockingly true. Feel free to enjoy them in sequential order or by which interests you most. All I hope for is that you jump on the train...

# It All Starts Here
## Growing Up Is a Bitch

My childhood trauma is not something I wanted to revisit. However, it is part of who I am. As a child, my mother noticed my mind worked differently than my older brother's and the other kids around me. I could remember colors and shapes, but I was unresponsive to anything mundane. She said I would laugh when she showed me colored blocks, not so with plain ones. I always wanted things in order, although this impulse has lessened over time. The comforting touch of fabric could magically make me stop crying. These quirks may be why I was attracted to my first real jobs, a harbinger of the development of my career as a nonconformist businessman.

Growing up, we never had money. Not as I understand it today. I thought if you lived in a house, you were rich. My family rented a two-bedroom, one-bath apartment. Our family of five lived there for over fifteen years. My parents shared a bedroom, as did my brother and me, and my sister got the living room.

I didn't feel poor. I felt middle class. Everyone was the same where I grew up. It was a Jewish community where religious services were held in a parking garage used as a synagogue rather than an elaborate temple. Eventually, the parishioners got together and built a beautiful synagogue, which took years to complete. I was proud to be part of this community.

I don't know why, but clothing seemed to define everyone, which I liked. This was just an observation I had as a kid. It was obvious women understood this concept of fashion and men didn't.

As a preteen, I was overweight and struggled with a negative self-image because of it. I was teased and ridiculed in school. It was made worse because it began even before school started—at home—at the relentless hands and mouth of my older brother, Howard.

He and I were typical of brothers everywhere, constantly in the seesaw throes of a love-hate relationship. We fought nonstop and schemed mischievous brotherly plots against each other. I once gave him a laxative disguised as a gift of chocolate candy, and not long afterward he thoughtfully made a salami sandwich for me loaded with screaming hot Chinese mustard plastered inside.

It was all common brotherly tyranny and cemented our long-running relationship as best friends and business partners. The strength of our relationship surely steeled us for the ups and downs we would encounter together. He was always the smart one, sometimes too smart for his or my good. I was slow in school. He became an accountant like my father. He hated it and later became an immigration lawyer and my partner in numerous businesses.

At age sixteen, I knew I had to change my entire approach to living as I began to enter manhood. It was 1961, and the world was changing too. I didn't want to be picked on for being overweight any longer. I began exercising. I went on every diet invented. I was going to fight this problem.

At first, nothing worked with my self-directed weight loss program. I began to take diet pills, which were common in those days. There must have been some ad in the newspaper that promised miracles, the "safe and easy way." I did it on the sly—no one knew I was doing this. And I began to shed weight. A lot of weight. I felt like a new person, filled with confidence and energy.

Later, when I found out that these pills were the same as amphetamines (speed) and not good for you, I became conflicted: do I give up the pills and go back to the way I was, or do I continue taking the pills and live my new, better life? Like many, I succumbed to the quick cure they advertised and continued to take the diet pills despite learning that they were not at all safe. Taking the easy way out is most often not the best way to go, but it sure is tempting. My developing vanity was calling the shots. I'm still vain so many years later!

Around this time, I was diagnosed as manic-depressive. Without disclosing this, the story of my life would not be complete or fully true. More importantly, I hope to provide encouragement for those living with hidden disorders to seek support and treatment.

Even today, there is fear of being treated as damaged goods and marked as less valuable than others. I'm here to tell you that those affected are not and neither am I. With proper diagnosis, treatment, and care, you're capable of thriving and accomplishing your dreams.

For those unaware of bipolar disorder (as it is now called) and how it impacts lives, let me explain what that means from a first-person viewpoint. Untreated, people experience tremendous, often euphoric highs (manic) and can swing into equally tremendous lows (depressive). You can't control when these shifts happen. They just take over and guide your behavior. That doesn't mean that you can't function, though. When you're low, you try to hide as if everything is normal. The highs, on the other hand, can get you in trouble. Because you think you're stronger, smarter, and more intuitive than those around you. You're so sure of yourself that you can make some really bad decisions and big mistakes. I don't want to neglect the depression side. I was lucky to be able to hide it, but for others it can be paralyzing.

In my case, I began to find myself thinking and acting unusually. I became paranoid, thinking that people were watching me. Things seemed to go in and out of focus; colors started changing. I began thinking my parents were my enemies—even more than my brother. They became very concerned and took me to see one psychiatrist and then another, looking for answers and help.

I have grim, vivid memories of this time. Eventually, my parents took me into a dark, brick building with few windows. It was at the intersection of Grand Central Parkway and Queens Boulevard. It was up on a hill, with a circular driveway, as I recall. To me at the time, it seemed to have a dark, ominous cloud suspended over it. It was frightening. In the years since then, I've looked for that building—it no longer exists; it's now condominiums. As a real estate developer who drives change, I find that ironic.

Back then, mental illness was a stigma and everything about it was kept in the unspoken shadows. The dark brick building was a hospital of some sort, and I had no idea why I was there. In accordance with the acceptable treatment of that time, they performed shock therapy on me with my parents' consent. This is where my memory becomes a bit murky.

To this day, I remember just parts of the experience. I do recall that my arms, wrists, and ankles were strapped to a flat table; a blinding light shone in my face; and three or four blurred figures were hovering over me. I was crying and screaming the whole time. Then they put a rubber ball in my mouth, held in by a rubber strap. I remember crying silently then. At that point, I think they put me under anesthesia. I remember a metal bonnet of some fashion connected to two wires. That's everything I recall.

When I woke up, my mouth was sore, and my head was foggy and empty. Then my parents collected me and took me home. I was told that the whole "treatment" took place in just one morning, but I really had no gauge of time. For all I know, it could have been a day or even a week.

As a teen, I worked in retail. My mother never hesitated to let me know she thought it was a dead end. After I was home for two weeks recovering from this barbaric ordeal, she got me a job in an office. I was expected to do clerical work despite my mind still being foggy from the shock therapy. Compounded with my dyslexia, the organizational tasks I was given were nearly impossible to accomplish.

At that time, I was only aware of my struggles and not the condition. (More on how this deeply affected my life and career will follow.) It was a complete disaster, as you can imagine. I didn't stand a fat chance, and I made a mess of the place in a short time. I wouldn't be surprised if they never recovered.

Despite the promises, the shock therapy procedure wasn't helping me. My parents wouldn't give up trying to find proper care for me. They brought me to one therapist after another, none of which worked though. At every meeting, they all asked the same questions for about fifteen minutes. Then we sat in silence until the end of my session.

One day, my relentless mother took me to see Dr. Alan Cott. When we went to his office, I immediately noticed that it was different from all the others. Everything was perfectly in place and organized. It was wonderfully styled in a trendy way, and it appealed to my sense of aesthetics and design. I noticed everything.

In Dr. Cott's private office, the stylish interior decor theme continued. He sat at a perfectly honed, rectangular desk with a black suede desk pad. He had one single drawer that held his patients' folders for the day. On top of his desk were four pencils without erasers, perfectly sharpened. When he walked into the room and we met him, he was personally as well put together as his office. Minimalistic and immaculate in dress, he was a small man with a large head hidden by short, coiffed hair. He reminded me of a Hollywood movie star from that era; he even spoke like one.

He reviewed my blood work. You always had to draw blood at his lab, two weeks prior to each session. Initially, I saw him four times, and then once a year unless I had an unusual problem. Dr. Cott determined that my problem was an imbalance of chemicals in the blood, possibly a result of the pills I had taken. "We'll get you back in balance and you will be good as new," he said confidently.

I trusted him and felt relieved, I remember. Determining the right prescription for treating an individual is the hardest part of a cure and it's all done by trial and error. In my case, at that time, Dr. Cott prescribed a mega dose of the vitamin niacin. Over those first four weeks of visits, I was back to normal, thinking clearly and coming out of the fog. It felt like a miracle.

There was one side effect of the niacin treatment, though. Your blood would seemingly rush to the surface of your skin, and you would get very hot and look like you had a bad, very red sunburn. That was a minor problem it seemed because it didn't last long. I learned to take the treatments privately and wait for the redness to stop before heading out in public. One time I took it just before entering an elevator on a high floor. When we got to the lobby, everyone was looking at my blazing red skin. To this day I don't know what they must have thought.

By now, I was feeling good and firing on all cylinders when I got a call from Dr. Cott himself. This was a first. It seems that high doses of niacin were taken off the market by the government, and I wouldn't be able to use it anymore. He said he had been experimenting with a new drug that he felt would work, but we can experiment just as we had done initially, he noted. The new drug was lithium. It has proved to be a miraculously remarkable and effective treatment for sufferers of bipolar disease, including myself.

If you or someone you love lives with doubts and fears about their disabilities, I hope to inspire you to seek remedies that are available—there are medical professionals who ply their craft with sincere compassion and care. Like Dr. Cott, they can help find the proper treatments to improve your quality of life.

As for myself, when I look back on my life and career, viewed from the prism of my disabilities, I can see that success is multifaceted. I somehow never considered myself successful, but by perseverance my brother and I had more hits than misses. We lived up to our parents' old-fashioned notion that to earn enough money to live comfortably and care for our families was the measure of success. From that perspective, we've honored their wishes.

In the end, it is the nurtured relationships with family and loved ones that I value most. I miss my brother. He passed while I was writing this book. I wish he were still here to see how valuable his contributions and our resolute care for each other, against all odds, have positively impacted so many other lives throughout our long journey together. I know he would be proud.

## The Leisure Suit ②
Men's Freedom through Fashion

### 1971

America is rumbling. Richard Nixon is president. The Vietnam War continues to rage. The counterculture is growing, getting more restless and more aggressive. New York City is crumbling under Mayor John Lindsay. Crime, graffiti, and squeegee guys pop up everywhere. Times Square is squalid and X-rated. Beatle George Harrison's Concert for Bangladesh is attended by 40,000 at Madison Square Garden. Fashion is becoming a statement against the establishment: Bell-bottoms, the Mod craze from England, Woodstock, flower power, and the Nehru jacket. Time to jump on the train.

### Lenny The Shop Owner
Fashion was a natural place for me to apply my creative self.

Unsurprisingly, my first job was in a men's clothing store. I began working in a couple of clothing stores when I was in high school and college. It was a pivotal time in my development and led me to understand that I would need to rely upon myself to create opportunities.

I was working at two different men's clothing stores at the time. Roger Garett, next to the historic RKO movie theater in Flushing, Queens, and The Elliot Shop, just east in the hamlet of Manhasset. The owner of Roger Garett was named Lenny, and we catered to artists, beauticians, and those of questionable occupations.

Lenny looked like a cartoon character with exaggerated features. From the waist up, he appeared tall and strong but had toothpick legs that didn't fit his frame. He was always hitching up his pants just like a cartoon character might comically do.

Lenny dressed like a gangster and tried to act the part, but he was far from one. Maybe it was simply because he sold clothing that catered to that clientele.

He gave me freedom to do things in the store such as "trimming" the display windows, which I became quite good at. I innovated and began to create a buzz around the neighborhood.

I had mannequins sitting suggestively on men's laps; two men dressed "to the nines" in suit and tie posed as wrestlers. At other times, I even had small live animals roaming around the mannequins. I created a sexy and provocative (for those times, anyway) window that grabbed eyeballs—a *Psycho* movie shower scene window, à la Alfred Hitchcock. Lenny began to really like what I was doing with the scenes, and I enjoyed the freedom to exercise my creativity.

The windows brought in women to buy gifts for their men, and they also purchased men's clothing for themselves while they were there. Maybe that was the beginning of unisex dressing!

I also fitted everyone who needed alterations. You take a piece of tailor chalk and mark the garment, so the tailors know what alterations need to be made. It's a real skill and a good tailor won't let you do it if you're not skillful at it.

Thinking back on that period, I was working three different jobs, all within the same week. Roger Garrett, The Elliot Shop, and at Jan's, a diner on Queens Boulevard. I wasn't keeping up with school. I really enjoyed being constantly busy.

School was slow, and I wasn't happy—I needed the action of talking to people. I really loved being with people, and I could absorb knowledge from them. For me, school wasn't working. I took the most active shifts at both stores and worked at the restaurant on Sundays, the busiest day of the week there.

## Abe and Elliot

At The Elliot Shop, I learned what rich was. The kids were spoiled. The parents were very demanding. Everything had to be perfect. Abe and Elliot owned the store.

Abe was the older of the two partners. Elliot was unruly and difficult to deal with. Elliot's father, who was an old friend of Abe's, had brought the two together. They built one of the finest men's stores on the East Coast.

They had been open about five years when I first came on the scene. I got along with Abe outstandingly—Elliot not so much.

My work there aligned with pretty much everything I did at Roger Garrett; except they didn't let me dress the windows. They had a professional company do that, and the result was very button-downed and staid. It was not to my taste at all.

One day, to my surprise, Abe came over to me and said, "I want you to take over my part of the store." I was shocked. I was only twenty-three years old. Abe said he wanted to retire and didn't trust Elliot to run it alone.

At first, I thought he was kidding. When I realized he was serious, I started to lose sleep thinking about being partners with Elliot.

Did I want to take advantage of this opportunity? Abe said he would lend me the money, and I could pay it back over time. My father was always wary of debt. This stuck in the back of my mind. He said the banks would always give you enough rope to hang yourself. I carried his sentiment throughout my career with some exceptions.

Even with Abe offering to set me up in the business, I realized that I just couldn't do it. It would be too much pressure. Maybe I was missing the train and Abe was offering me the ticket.

I learned an important lesson. I said no. At this point, I realized I was wasting my time working as I did. It was a dead end, and I knew it. Suddenly, I saw a much bigger world out there, and I was going to jump in. I was going to get on the train.

After turning away from the offer to become Elliot's partner, I looked at money very differently. I remember thinking that the real money is in wholesale. It seemed that all the salesmen who sold suits to the stores in those days made out very well; it was like printing money. So, it seemed, anyway.

The salesmen would come into the store with their assistant rolling a huge and impressive-looking garments rack. It was all very ceremonious, and it caught my attention.

Either Elliot or Abe would meet them, sometimes together. They would always have lunch, and the salesman would always leave with an order of some sort.

Lunch seemed like the most important meal of the day in business. (Eventually that became breakfast.) That's when I knew I had to break into the men's clothing market as a salesman, just like the guys I was watching so closely.

And that's when I also learned what the word nepotism meant. The senior salesmen would always pass their accounts to their children. It was standard family practice unless the kid was a jerk, but that was rare.

So, with no apparent way of breaking into that field, I broadened the search and began studying the classified ad section of the *New York Times*. It certainly seems quaint now, but that's where you looked for jobs in those days.

## Richard

I arranged an interview and went to an address off 7th Avenue. It was a low building with many showrooms on each floor, one right after the other. None had any distinguishing features. I was instructed to go to suite A1945. I remember that number because that's the year I was born.

When I walked into the office, the place was a mess everywhere I looked. There were randomly placed ladies' dresses on racks, counters, and even the floor. Only one person was in the office—the owner Richard.

Richard was from Texas. He was nice enough but clearly very nervous; you could just tell he was uncomfortable about everything. Richard could not give orders; in fact, he found it hard to finish most sentences.

Buyers visiting the showroom had the same impression I did. I was always getting looks from the buyers as if to say, "Is he really the boss?" Richard was relieved to have someone take the attention off him—even me, the new kid, who didn't really know what I was selling.

Pointing to the showroom, Richard explained that the place was a mess because of his last showing. I noticed that the dresses hung as if they were window curtains. They were BIG!

Some had large flower prints and looked like the whole garden could have been there. He said these were half-size dresses—a comical euphemism I had never heard of before, but they were indeed huge. Surprisingly so.

I always considered myself aware of fashion, but this was unlike anything I'd ever seen. Richard began to explain there was a very large demand for this type of clothing.

As he was talking, I made a mental note that I needed a job, and if there was a big demand for these big garments, I could make some money selling them. What the heck? So now I was a dress salesman and a half-size dress salesman to boot!

It didn't sound all that bad, actually, at least not until I met the department store buyers at places like Macy's and Lord & Taylor. They were all attractive, shapely young women in petite-size dresses, and it was immediately clear to me that they were not happy being the buyers of these draperies masquerading as women's dresses. They had a distasteful attitude toward me for the audacity of selling them.

Nonetheless, I tried to date one or two of these buyers, maybe even all of them! I was young. No one would go out with me, not even for coffee. I hated constantly being personally rejected, but they bought a lot of the dresses, so it wasn't a total loss.

I stuck it out with Richard for over six months. I learned a lot, and I was making good money, but I knew this wouldn't, couldn't become my life's work. It just didn't feel right. It felt like a step down.

### Sid

One day, Sid and I were alone in the elevator of my building. He sold fabric to Tribute Dress, Richard's operation. I had seen him in the showroom a few times. He bluntly asked if I was happy at Tribune. I told him, equally bluntly, that I hated it.

Sid was very slick. Back in the day, we used to say you have to count your fingers after shaking hands with a guy like Sid. But I think everyone has met a character like him. He told me that he could get me a training job in the textile company and teach me the business. He arranged an interview for me at his company, Wolesco.

### Lester Cohen

That's how I met Lester Cohen. He was the president of this division of Wohlschlaeger, the parent company. Lester was a handsome, worldly looking gentleman with a striking tight crop of white hair. He was tight in other ways, too: physically, with money, and he possessed a rigid personality.

I felt Lester could easily pick your pocket while smiling straight at you. Sinister sophistication, it seemed to me. It was my first experience with meeting an actual wolf in sheep's clothing.

Lester wouldn't turn out to be the last such wolf I would meet in my career, and I found out quickly that they come in all shapes and sizes. They're not always easy to see, but to survive in the business world, it's essential that you recognize the wolves quickly. They're everywhere.

Lester was the big boss. He even controlled the owner of the parent company. No one ever wanted to end up on his wrong side. He would walk around the office and berate a different salesman every day. He thought that was good training for them. Tough love, Lester-style, I guess.

I was going to be trained in the textile industry—actually, really trained for the first time ever—or so I thought. It wasn't exactly as advertised. It was more of a bait and switch. My "training" consisted of sitting at a desk in the storage room, day-after-day cutting swatches for the sales force. That was it!

I had to cut fabric so the salespeople could leave samples with customers. Cutting fabric all day was worse than selling half-size dresses—at least at Tribune I met pretty girls!

## Arthur Wolshleger

Then I met Arthur, the only lucky aspect of the job. Arthur

Wohlschlaeger, the namesake and head of the parent company, was always coming into the storage room. He would come in at lunchtime, and we would eat together. He would talk about a yacht he was building in Europe to compete in the America's Cup, the international sailboat race that dates back to the mid-eighteen hundreds.

I knew Arthur liked me, because he told me so, and he was now actually training me. It seemed more like a father-and-son relationship, just like with the owners of the clothing stores. With Arthur's good training and wisdom under my belt and the confidence that goes with it, I told him I was ready to go out and sell.

He told me I had to go to Lester and tell him what I wanted to do. He apologized, saying sheepishly that he had no influence in that division. I'm sure that he was afraid of Lester. As I noted earlier, Lester was the Boss of The Boss. I think Arthur put in a good word for me, but I'm not sure. If he did, though, that might have worked against me with Lester.

Throughout this whole learning period—including the dress business—I continued to work weekends and Thursday nights in the two clothing stores. I finally gave up my job at the restaurant. Here's why: I didn't like their business practices. They were fine with cheating customers and that was not okay with me.

On one occasion, a customer I had just served said that the check was wrong—that it was too much. I had indeed inadvertently overcharged, by a lot, and it was clearly my mistake. The owner, who was working the register, profusely apologized to the customer, but when he left, instead of admonishing me, said, "Nice try, maybe you'll do better next time." It was his smile that got to me. Another smiling wolf. I quit then and there.

## Saul Hirsh

Now I had to earn more money, so I went to Lester Cohn and said I wanted to go out and sell. I was ready. I said I saw a fabric that I was sure I could sell. Lester was very dismissive, as always, but over days and weeks of me working on him, he finally said okay. I must have worn him down.

He told me I had to find and train my replacement. I agreed, and he reduced my pay initially because he said I wouldn't produce anything for the company at first. He was right and I agreed. My new job was to assist Saul Hirsh, a salesman well past his better years.

Saul was a heavyset man in his seventies, and he used a very large magnifying glass to aid his vision. Saul was a fantastic character and larger than life to me in some ways. His stories were consistently over the top.

He said he knew politicians, celebrities, and everyone in the whole industry personally. Even though he was very convincing, most customers thought he was full of beans, yet they liked doing business with him and loved his stories.

To this day, I'm sure Saul was the most experienced person in any field that I've ever met. That's a big statement for me—I've met a lot of smart people.

I always appreciated how my young age played a part in my success. Saul took me under his wing as Abe, Arthur, and Lenny had, but with the finesse of a deeper relationship. And it grew deeper all the time. I was Saul's eyes, and now he used the magnifying glass only on occasion. It signified trust, and I thrived on it. I'll share more about Saul, but his story is worth a book of its own.

One day I showed Saul the fabric that I felt I could sell to the menswear market. He said he thought that could work. I had never even been to a menswear showroom, but Saul said, "Go for it. It's your time." But first, I had to persuade Lester Cohn again to let me try.

They had never considered menswear a viable market. When I approached Lester, who was with Sid, the guy who originally got me into the company, they both laughed. Hard. But they curiously asked me to show them the piece of fabric as if I were selling them. It felt like an audition, so that's what I did.

After the presentation, their exact words were: "You know nothing about fabric, and all you have is a glib tongue."

I didn't know what glib meant, so initially, I thought it was a good sign.

Then, Sid said, "Give the kid a shot."

I guess he must have felt guilty about misrepresenting this "training" program.

Immediately, Lester said, "Alright, but you're no longer on salary." He explained that he would give me a $50 decrease in salary and put me on a draw against a 6-percent commission once I reached over $125,000 in sales. Part of the deal was that I would have to take care of all my expenses.

I went to Saul and asked what he thought. He said that was a very high commission rate, and that he didn't trust Lester.

"What do you have to lose?" he said. "Time? At your age, you have plenty of that to spare." He said this in a discernibly melancholy tone.

I consider this to be the best advice I've ever received. I accepted the deal and started right away that following Monday.

Now, I had a rude awakening: How in the world would I sell this fabric? After all, no one had ever used it for men's clothing. It certainly didn't help that no one in that market knew me from a hole in the wall. I was nobody with a product that no one knew they wanted or needed.

## Angelo

I was working in Abe's men's store that weekend, so I asked this mentor what he thought, and he said to ask Angelo. Angelo was the head of the tailoring department at the store—a vital position in a clothing store. Angelo was possibly the most difficult person I'd ever met.

Angelo created that same fear in all the salesmen, even the owners of the store. But I knew I needed his talent, and he was a highly skilled artisan tailor. They aren't easy to find. With some trepidation, I asked Angelo to make a garment I had in mind from that new piece of fabric I had been thinking about.

Little did I know that he took my request as a great compliment. From that moment on, Angelo treated me like family—like a son. The work he did on my garment was fantastic. It was as good as I had envisioned. Maybe even better. My youthful enthusiasm was working in my favor!

Before I knew it, I was standing at the door of 1290 Avenue of the Americas carrying a bag with a blue-and-white-striped jacket along with swatches of color samples. This building was the center of the menswear industry. Every major manufacturer of importance had offices and showrooms at 1290 Avenue of the Americas.

The lobby was an impressive modern structure with very high ceilings. There were fifteen elevators, and there was activity and motion everywhere. Buyers from all over the country came here to stock their stores with items they hoped would fly off their shelves.

I started by looking at the index of tenants on the lobby wall. Looking at the list, I realized I knew most of these vendors from both clothing store jobs I'd worked. Bubbling with enthusiasm, seeing buyers was going to be fun, I thought. That bubble popped as soon as I made my first presentation. They were not impressed. At all.

I then made five more presentations without a request for one single sample. I went home wishing I had taken Abe up on his offer to become a partner in The Elliot Shop and felt comforted knowing that I would be at the store the following Thursday night.

The next day was the same. This went on for weeks. Then something happened. One of the first manufacturers who turned me down told one of his buyers about me. It was a very tight industry. That day went very well, as did the weeks that followed. Everyone was asking for samples and sample swatches. But that was it—all I was doing was sampling, and you don't make any money just giving away samples.

Lester started to become upset—that was easy for him to do. Saul said to hang in there. The expenses were eating up all my money. Saul said I should put in for taking customers to lunch, but I said I couldn't afford that. Don't worry, Saul said encouragingly, "Make up the first one, a little white lie, and the rest will follow. You're gonna be okay."

Lester's face got red every time I put in a request for expenses. He'd say, "I'm adding it to your draw," noting that all I did was book free samples and write no "paper," no orders. It was a losing proposition. So, every morning, I became an easy target for Lester's ranting. He said that it was only because of Saul that he had let it go on so long. He said he would have fired me weeks ago. Lester didn't mince words.

The womenswear fashion industry was controlled by the seasons, and it cut the seasons into sections. There wasn't just spring and fall seasons—there were at least six collections. If you could survive in that industry, you could survive anything, it seemed. I didn't have the nerve for that pressure cooker. I did understand the men's industry, which was more old-school, more like a regular business.

I was about to change things around in the fashion world. In a BIG way. I took a womenswear "Warp Knit" fabric and brought it to the conservative menswear industry. I didn't plan to rattle the men's fashion world, but a disruption is exactly what happened.

All I wanted to do was make a name for myself and get men out of those ubiquitous corporate uniforms. You know, the navy suit with the striped tie and white shirt that legions of men wore like uniforms day-in-and-day-out. I felt it was time for men to get comfortable, to have more things to choose from, to be individuals and basically to have the freedom of personal style. Just like the women had.

My lack of actual orders was about to go away with a loud bang. I was the only salesman being harassed daily by Lester Cohen. He kept saying I was wasting his time. I believed that the orders would come, but I clearly had no experience or guarantees to offer. I sure did have a lot of heart and desire to succeed, though.

## The Breakthrough

Then it happened I got my first order. It was a brand-new small manufacturer. The order was a total of just $500, but it sure felt big to me. Lester didn't say a single word—he just smirked. Then just two-weeks later the menswear industry bought about half of my draw that week. It was a veritable flood of orders. This brought a breath of fresh air to a very tired industry. I did a whopping $50,000 worth of business that month.

That surely attracted Lester's attention. He came out that following day and said uncharacteristically, "Congratulations." Then he said, "Let's you and I go up and see some of your customers." I had no choice but to comply. He was my boss.

Lester was like a fish out of the water when he wasn't yelling at salespeople. He just didn't have the people skills needed to engage well with customers and that's not something you can fake. My customers knew his type and did not treat him well at all. That may have been sparked by my telling them stories about him, never thinking they would meet.

Mercifully, Lester realized right away that he didn't belong on sales calls because he never asked to go with me again. Everyone began to say that he was lucky to have me. He would visibly cringe at these comments.

As we went back to the office, Lester said, "I'm going to change your deal. You know that deal that I made with you when

I let you go out and sell?" I nodded yes. "Well, that's an unheard-of deal in the industry," he continued. There was a long, uncomfortable pause. "I'll tell you what I'm going to do: I'll raise your salary to $150 a week and give you a big bonus at Christmas." I thought to myself that I couldn't say anything because he was The Boss. I was at his mercy.

I didn't know it at the moment, but Lester changed my entire life right then because he didn't honor his word about our deal. From that very first order, they continued to roll in like the tide: I sold $1.2 million that first season. It was an astounding success and proved that my crazy idea worked. Putting a pencil to it, I would have earned over $65,000, the equivalent of nearly $500,000 in 2023. Because Lester changed our deal, all he paid me, including the holiday bonus, was $8,800. I wasn't happy with Lester's underhanded approach to success in this new market, and I gave my notice six months later after making sure that all my orders were shipped to my customers.

Lester tried to offer me more money to stay, but it was far too late for that. I snidely suggested that he should go up to 1290 7th Avenue himself and that I was sure that he would be greeted there with open arms.

He never did that, of course, but he did send Saul. The only thing that Saul handled were prints for shirtings. I happily opened doors for Saul, and I told people how much he had helped me. They never did business with my fabrics from Wolesco, but Saul did very well with one of my best customers.

## Burlington Industries

A customer of mine had told someone at Burlington Industries, one of the largest textile mills in the country, about me. He must have said some nice things because it was more like a tour with a sell than an interview when I arrived. They had a large menswear division that sold woven fabrics. They only sold knits to the women's market.

Everyone at Burlington was clean-shaven and wore black suits with striped ties. This Burlington uniform certainly didn't fit my style. I stood out like a sore thumb. I had a mustache—soon to become a full beard. I wore a sports jacket and nonmatching pants and sneakers. I certainly stuck out with my nonconformity, only now in the middle of a corporate machine.

That first day, everyone seemed to stare at me—secretaries, mail clerks, every salesperson, even the executives. They all seemed nice, but they just didn't know what to make of me. I was given a desk in a room by myself. I wouldn't call it an office. It was more like a huge closet with a small window. It was clearly a step up from Wolesco, however. I was making progress!

For a few days, I just took in the lay of the land. From there, my relationships with my customers from the 1290 building began to pay off. Good relationships sure go a long way in the corporate world, and Burlington personified the corporate world in those days.

Within a couple of months, I was back in the groove of taking samples to the menswear building. Something I saw struck me. I don't remember when I saw the first double-knit fabric, but I think it was when I took the time to look at the lines of all the divisions. On one of the racks in Burlington's womenswear department I saw this knit fabric that would change everything; I could feel it. Little did I know that this was the genesis of the leisure suit.

I brought the fabric to the store and asked my now good friend Angelo to make a suit, but only with shirt lapels instead of normal suiting lapels. In my vision, it had to look completely different. A game-changer.

Angelo thought I had lost my mind for sure, but just like a friend would do, he made it for me. It came out great, and I got excited with the possibilities.

So, I went to the head of the womenswear department and asked how much volume they did with this fabric. Not much, he said. Burlington didn't have its own equipment to make the fabric. After asking what price they sell it for, I took that price, added 20 percent, and began to offer it to my customers.

I showed my unusual new suit, and everyone sampled the fabric. Anticipating sales starting to kick in, I told the head of the women's wear department that I would need fabric soon. They had bought it from other mills and resold it to their customers. I just didn't expect this from one of the largest mills in the country.

## Clara Hancock

I was opening a whole new market. You could just smell the fresh opportunities. All the clothing manufacturers flipped over this unique style even before they had shown it to their buyers. The retail customers would be the real judge, though. They always are.

One day I was with one of my favorite manufacturers in his showroom. In walked Clara Hancock, then the most influential writer for *Men's Wear Daily*, the industry's largest trade paper. Everyone read Clara. She was smart and well respected. Almost a deity in the business. She saw me holding my garment, and without missing a beat, she spoke her magic words: "This will sell. I'll call it the 'Leisure Suit,'" she prophetically added.

That's how it all started, with one well-placed newspaper story by Clara Hancock. Soon, Johnny Carson began wearing the leisure suit on *The Tonight Show*, and we were off and running. From that point on, I didn't sleep for six years, it seemed.

Everyone wanted a leisure suit. It changed the men's fashion world. It changed cultural perceptions, too. There were pages and pages of press and even major stories in multiple issues of *GQ*. It was a true phenomenon, and I was its creator.

Overnight, the leisure suit replaced conventional men's fashion. Now, you wouldn't wear a regular suit in a restaurant or at a party. That was for the "squares."

Initially, manufacturers didn't know how to make leisure suits or even where to get the unusual double-knit fabric. There was a limited inventory of the fabric, which only added to the demand. Every manufacturer wanted to get on the bandwagon and make some money.

The success of many manufacturers depended on this style. Some even tried to make it in different fabrics that fell flat. The newness of the double-knit fabric was the key to the success of the leisure suit. Every knitting mill got into the act, even underwear and T-shirt knitters.

I learned early on that to truly be successful, you must think beyond what you know. I knew I had to create something that would be unique and draw attention. Well, I did, and I soon found my new idea copied everywhere you looked. My leisure suit was what was called "a hit." A big hit, actually.

Unfortunately, the fashion industry is notorious for stealing ideas. They're called knockoffs. When great designers complained, they were shunned even by the stores. If "Imitation is the greatest compliment," it usually benefits the sellers, not the creators. The fashion industry moved very quickly then—still does—and there's little time to protect a design because there's always another trend nipping at its heels.

Imagine a new item hits the market and makes everything else obsolete. Then everybody wants it, tries to buy it, and can't find it.  This is how fads begin to grow wildly. Prices began to go through the roof and the whole textile industry was turned upside down. It kept building.

Celebrities started to walk the red carpet dressed in leisure suits. That only added to the demand. I was a very busy guy. Haggar Clothing wanted to buy my entire yearly production. I said thank you, but no. I'm not sure that anyone had ever said no to Jim Haggar, the company's founder—he was one of the most powerful men in the industry. But I wasn't willing to put all my eggs in one basket. Even a big basket like Haggar.

At this time, I had twenty-one salesmen over the country, a full back-office staff, and two secretaries to manage office traffic. It was 1971 and I was earning $35,000 a year and doing very well. I decided to travel around the country to meet all the new and happy customers.

I brought my girlfriend's Nikon camera on my trips to take

pictures of all the company owners. I told them it was to put them in my "rogues' gallery." I didn't realize what a big success the rogues' gallery was becoming. I would send them all a print of their photo as well as those of the complete gallery. We were in the Brotherhood Club together!

I also didn't realize that many of these businessmen had never seen or knew much about many of their competitors. I used the gallery to remember everyone I met. I took a picture of Jim Haggar. He was second only to Farrah Pants, which was the largest. For some reason, Mr. Farrah didn't let me take his picture. I guess he didn't want to be in the rogues' gallery with the rest of us.

In one year, astoundingly for the time, we did over $20 million in business. We used the production capacity of most of the knitting machines in the country to achieve that level of volume. I'm sure we would have done $40 million had I stayed, and I was expecting a huge bonus—but neither was to be.

During this hectic period, I worked 24/7/365. I was consumed with feeding the fire I had built. I was designing the fabric, selling, and portioning who got the production because of the limited supply. I thought I was a rock star, but I would be brought back to earth very quickly.

I finally found out how corporations really operated. There had been a shakeup of the top brass of the company. The board had demoted my rabbi, a mentor who protected me and helped me maintain my unusual autonomy. I soon realized the next stop on this amazing ride was not going to be with Burlington. They were not buying any equipment or making an investment. I realized big corporations have no feelings for their people, or at least that's what I saw at Burlington, as you will see.

Burlington's new president had no personality whatsoever. I met with him in a small, nondescript room. He got to the point of the meeting quickly.

"We are going to eliminate the men's knit division," he said.

I responded, "What are you doing? We have done so much business!"

"That's the problem. You're hurting all our other men's divisions," he said.

The new president told me that I had to fire my entire salesforce—twenty-one men with families who relied on them.

I responded with great bravado, "Make that twenty-two."

He didn't flinch. He wasn't bothered at all. It was clearly time to move on, but I had the bravery of the winds of success filling my wings now. No matter what happened, I was going to be alright, I thought.

## Big Move, Bad Press

Moving quickly, I joined with two other Burlington people to discuss what to do. We planned to set up our own company. We searched for a financial partner and made our plans to leave Burlington.

I was about to be unemployed, and this was startling after the grand successes we had garnered. Still moving quickly—and not wanting to miss a beat—I went again to the industry sage Clara Hancock and told her that three executives that head the Burlington knit division were leaving to set up their own company called

Brooke Industries. We picked that name because we thought it had an old Southern or English feel to it. (What would you expect from three Jewish guys from Brooklyn!?) I never imagined that news—with Clara Hancock's byline—was going to be on the newsstands the next day.

When I went to work that day, the receptionist told me I would not be allowed in my office without a security guard present. My future partners were given the same abrupt news and treated the same way.

Now we were all out of jobs and on the street. My new partners were not happy with me, and it gave them second thoughts. Strong second thoughts. I felt like I screwed up by letting the cat out of the bag with Clara Hancock. I should have known that she would find this very newsworthy to our industry.

I tried to explain to my partners that we, our entire division, were going to be fired anyhow, and that the big boss told me that directly. They kind of forgave me. Moving on, we took a hotel room at the McAlpin Hotel right across the street from Burlington House as our new office.

Many of my customers had seen the Clara Hancock story and were calling to wish me well. I took advantage of the good press, and I contacted all my customers directly. It was a great launching pad for the new company. The three of us started in earnest to put the business together.

We each had our own distinct skills and responsibilities—we were becoming a good team. I designed the line, Barney Feldman took care of the back office, and Joseph Canter worked directly with the mills—the same mills we used at Burlington. We knew the game, and everything was falling in place.

We were growing fast and went quickly from the hotel "office" into an apartment in a building across the street from our previous employer. Soon, we took another apartment. Then another, and another. When we left that building after a year or so, we had grown into eleven apartments. More meetings took place in the elevator than anywhere else. It was time to find a new home for our growing company.

## Mr. Knit

My good reputation happily followed me. I was now called Mr. Knit in the industry. I earned that appellation at Burlington by being somewhat outrageous in the ways that I promoted knits. After all, these were outrageous times.

One such promotion was an ad I wrote for a trade magazine with a headline that read, *"Everything You Wanted to Know About Knits (But were afraid to ask.)"* This was a shameless, direct knock-off of a very popular, culturally significant book of the times on the topic of sex, which was coming out from behind closed doors, so to speak. Both the book—and the ad—caused quite a stir!

The publicity was good for Burlington because it made them seem like leaders in the knitting market even though they had never owned a knitting machine. And, at that time, Milliken and J.P. Stevens, their main competitors, were spending millions on knitting equipment. I positioned Burlington to look strong and powerful.

Following that ad, I created another ad highlighting that we had printed a book listing the *Ten Most-Asked Questions and Answers*

*About Knits* because we had such an overwhelmingly positive response to our knits. I was the only one asking these questions!

To my surprise, we received requests for over 50,000 books. It was a huge success and created very powerfully strong PR for Burlington. I was featured in the book showing how knits just wouldn't wrinkle like woven fabrics. We produced it in-house and included an actual round-edge knitting needle that was required to sew knits properly.

All this promotion helped cement my reputation as Mr. Knit—a reputation that helped launch the new company so well. Burlington didn't even know what they were losing at the time. They had no idea.

## MGM: Our New Home

Still in need of more appropriate office space than our collection of apartments, I happened to cross the street to the MGM building on 55th Street. I asked one of the doormen if he knew of any office space that might be available. He said that MGM was moving to Las Vegas, leaving their executive offices on the twenty-first floor available. At the time, MGM was leaving the movie business and getting ready to open the MGM Grand Hotel.

I've found that NYC doormen know just about everything about their buildings, and I've relied on them for smart inside information throughout my career in real estate. The doorman added that MGM really wanted to get out of the lease, and it had been sitting on the market for some time.

I was pretty sure that we couldn't afford that space, but I met with the building manager to discuss it.

I got right to the point, "How much is the rent?"

He said, "You know it's ten-thousand square feet, don't you?"

I said I did, and he told me that it was priced at $3 a foot. My whole body became a bit unglued on the inside, but on the outside, I was like ice. I thought for sure there must be a mistake for the price to be that low.

I asked to see the space and told him right then it was more than I was willing to spend—my real estate negotiating skills were developing quickly—but that we needed to find new office space immediately.

We went up to see the 21st floor. I was prepared for the worst. As we got off the elevator, we were in a beautiful, fully finished reception area. I had this feeling of being in real, big-league executive offices just like in the movies. MGM movies, even!

The chairman's office was about 500 square feet on the northwest side of the floor. It had beautiful floor-to-ceiling palladium windows facing north and west, with a spectacular view of Central Park. The walls had beige real suede covering. The carpeting was plusher than in many fine homes. One wall was solid mahogany. I found out later there were two hidden doors behind that wall, one led to a full bar and the other a private bathroom with a shower.

It was all simply spectacular. As I walked with the manager, I kept straight-faced like a statue. I had a love of acting. So much so that I had taken some classes and even performed in local and college productions.

My past acting training was really paying dividends at that moment.

I ended up negotiating a bare-bones lease price for premier NYC office space. I was even able to purchase all the fine MGM furniture that remained there for a song. Talk about being in the proverbial "right-place-at-the-right-time." And I sure learned a lot about making moves in the world of NYC real estate, and that wisdom would come in very handy as my business future unfolded, as you'll see. In the end, this move catapulted our fledgling business into the stratosphere. Quickly.

Once we moved in and settled, I threw a large opening party that I knew would turn heads. And it did. Everyone came, including top designers such as Calvin Klein and Ralph Lauren. Just to name-drop a couple of them. Some of my friends and associates from Burlington came as well. Arthur was there. And Saul, too. I didn't invite Lester, but I was tempted to just for spite.

## Location, Location, Location

Between our innovations and the attention our company was receiving—and the audacious spectacle of moving into the MGM offices—we became a bona-fide destination for buyers from all over the country. Our new offices reeked of success, and they were instantly more impressive than all their other suppliers, including Burlington. And we were only across the street and a few blocks from the 1290 building. We were in the thick of the game, and it was a perfect setup in every way.

Every season from then on, we held fashion shows for our customers that lasted an entire week. They became must-attend destination events and helped us cement our position as a leader, playing a role in our exponential growth. We continued creating new ideas in the menswear industry. I hired the first woman salesperson in the field. She was smart, and an instant hit, and her sales were sure proof of that.

With everything we were doing, we were somehow doing better than we could afford to do. To grow a business, you need money, so that your operation can be capitalized properly. I was in my twenties, and I was learning how to run a business on the fly. I went to my financial partner and asked for advice. He had never expected this much success or the need for additional capital at this level. He was reluctant to invest more money. He suggested we do it the way everyone else in the textile world did business—they factored their receivables (that's lending like a bank but based on your orders).

One interesting back-office item was accounting. I learned there was a lot of wiggle room back there. I hired the most well-known, big-gun accounting firm in the textile business. With their name on my financial reports, the factor would never question anything.

In my second year, I realized how to really play the game: it was all about inventory. The more inventory (assets) you had, the more credit you got from the factors. The value of the inventory was the flexible item on the balance sheet. The value report was finalized over a fine lunch as was the accounting firm's fee for next year. This negotiation was one-sided. If I raised their yearly fee, I got the inventory value I wanted.

Our real inventory was predominantly yarn of all colors, old and new. I could put any number on this value so long as I didn't go over its cost. My values helped my balance sheet, and I got more credit. From that point on, I never believed a financial report again. That's why I don't trust the stock market and their reports—I just don't know who is having lunch with whom.

Years later, the accounting firm made a major mistake with a big company. They conjured an excellent valuation report for this large client so they could secure an equally large financing deal. The company abruptly turned belly-up and went bankrupt. The accounting firm was sued and promptly also went out of business. I learned that sometimes you just can't believe (or trust) what you're seeing.

## The Mill

We were buying all our goods from smaller mills, the same ones that Burlington used. In many cases, I gave these mills their start in menswear, and they remembered that and came to our aid more times than I can count. I've always been grateful for that.

Our quality-control foreman brought a gentleman into my office. His name was Mark. He said he could build a knitting mill for us with very little capital. The market was huge, and the profits were astounding. Knitting machines were complicated and very specialized and hard to come by, but if you could get one, it could pay for itself in six months, and it was all gravy from then on, profits, easy money.

There was one big problem—the amateurs' greed combined with lack of knowledge destroyed this legitimate market. I'll explain that more clearly later. Mark explained that the government was giving an investment tax credit with terms that were very attractive. He also said that North American Rockwell had fifty computerized knitting machines that they had no home for, and they had heard about Brooke Industries and our successes.

We were utilizing over 200 machines at several mills at the time. I had never heard of a computerized knitting machine before this. I was intrigued. These newfangled machines were amazing; they could make a pattern change yarn colors on what looked like a desktop computer, put it on tape, and copy the tape. The tape would run all the patterns the same and a pattern could not repeat for the tape's length, which was amazing. The computer machine was a tool for great design innovation and a production break-through. Rockwell had only sold a few of these new machines, and they needed exposure for their equipment.

Mark and I met with the head of this division, and, to my surprise, it was the Rockwell director himself. These guys were engineers through and through, with absolutely no knowledge of the fashion business. That's usually the case in many industries. The head of the division was not given much time to talk—the big boss wanted to put on the show.

He described their multimillion-dollar company and their many markets: aerospace, appliances, commuters, etc. So, I went into acting mode, telling them I always admired their company and how much I would love to work with them. I said that what they were trying to do in the design space was groundbreaking and very exciting. But production was entirely another matter, and it was a significant risk. That's not what they wanted to hear, and I could see Mark off to the side, cringing.

Then I changed gears and told them that what they really needed was a showcase to break into this market and that we were going to help them with just that. They were now paying close attention.

"I'm a risk-taker," I said. "We will open a mill, you will help us build it, and we will rent your machines for as long as we run them. We will pay for the equipment under a lease. If for any reason we stop running, you will take back the machines with no penalty."

I made up the deal as I spoke it. I was surprised when they accepted it just as I described. I can't even imagine how much money they had sunk into this division up to that point. They were desperate.

The nice part of this proposition was no mill had more than one computerized machine. These computers were very useful in design, and no one would know what we were doing. We would get a big jump and be first-to-market with this new technology. Also, we could reprogram all fifty machines overnight as market conditions changed. This was unheard of at the time.

Mark and I met with Rockwell again and worked out the details of the deal. We also got a government investment tax credit that was too good to pass up. So, we rented a 50,000-square-foot space in Lodi, New Jersey, and set up shop. It took about three months to become operational. With a four-month free rent incentive to set up, we paid very little for the mill, with Rockwell even paying half. Now Brooke Industries was a real, authentic mill. We owned more machines than Burlington. That surprised even me.

Mark ran the mill well and the fabric was top quality, delivered on time. He was a solid guy, I thought. The plant was running for about a year, and everything was going great. Gangbusters!, as they used to say. Smooth sailing is the time to be careful though, I've come to learn.

I could tell Mark was not happy, but I thought that he was having problems at home. He was always tight-lipped anyway. I moved my entire back office to Lodi and rented half of the floor at the old MGM space for $6 per square foot, which meant I was paying no rent for my offices in Manhattan plus I was making $3 per square foot for the company. This strategy would become a standby habit of mine throughout the years.

Then it happened. One day, Mark walked into my office and quit, just like that. It turns out he wanted to open another mill, and it was too good an opportunity to pass up, he said. I couldn't stop him.

I drove out to Lodi and met with Wolfgang, the second-in-charge. I told him he was now the number-one guy, to his surprise. I knew the rest of the crew—the good ones, and the ones you had to keep an eye on. At that point, everything seemed ready to run again smoothly without Mark.

One week after I took over the mill, a workman in overalls came into the reception area and asked to see me. He said that it was about the mill. I had never heard anything of him before. I was curious by then. After introductions, he stated he had been working with Mark. He wanted to know if I would be willing to keep the same arrangement as he had with Mark.

Arrangement? This was all new to me. Well, tell me about it, I most likely said. It all sounded fishy to me, and all I said was—not knowing what I was talking about—what are the numbers?

Most things in business revolve around numbers.

He started talking as though he was confessing. He said that in his agreement, he bought all the overruns of the fabric. He paid Mark $0.75 a pound for the waste. It seemed cheap—not a price I would have come up with, I don't think—and he explained why it wasn't. I said I needed to think about all this and ended the meeting. I did say I would call him with my thoughts before I did anything else.

I knew nothing about this arrangement, and I never once thought about the value of this waste. Mark surely did, though. After looking into it all, it turned out to be a sizable sum.

For starters, I don't particularly appreciate it when people steal from me. And then it got worse. I found out that Mark was also trying to take employees from my mill for his new project. I immediately called my attorney and started a lawsuit.

Before that, though, I called the overalls man into my office again. I interrogated him like I was the district attorney. I recorded everything he was saying surreptitiously with a Sony Walkman. He described how he paid Mark in cash but claimed he didn't record how much he had spent over three years, but it was around $3,000 a week, he figured. I said I wanted $0.90 a pound. He argued a bit but agreed to my new price.

Now I was prepared for the lawsuit against Mark. I had never initiated a suit before and only did so on one other occasion during my business career many years later. I quickly found out there were many legal fees in discovery before you had your day in court, so I played a little sleight of hand—I only sued for tortious interference in my business.

I would have won, I'm sure, but it would have taken far too long of a time and still hurt my mill. We started with my deposition, which went well. Then it was Mark's turn. I then asked the lawyers to leave the room, and they did so.

To my surprise, Mark brought his new partner into the room. He was a very wealthy investor from Lodi, and he had no textile experience whatsoever. We sat around my lawyers' large mahogany conference table, and I stated that everything in this meeting was off the record for now. I said I wanted to settle this dispute amicably, if possible, but I needed my men back or I would escalate the case to include criminal charges. Mark looked amused, but the investor was clearly shocked.

I said I wasn't fooling around and took out the Walkman. I placed it in the middle of the table and pushed the play button. Mark's face now began to turn colors, especially when the recording got to the part that said Mark didn't want anyone to know about this side deal. The investor seemed more uncomfortable by the second.

The recording had only played halfway when they heard the magic words of the overalls guy saying, "I paid Mark about $3,000 a week." Mark swallowed and asked if he could step outside the room. He and the investor went outside for a few minutes.

Only Mark returned. He said he would not take any men from my plant. As it turned out, he didn't need them. They never opened a knitting mill because the investor pulled out. That was that. The men came back to their jobs, but I never felt the same loyalty as I had before.

## Patchwork Denim

After that passed, it was back to running my business, but I needed a break. That whole incident took a lot out of me. I decided to go to Aspen to ski in the beautiful Rocky Mountains. There's one thing I've noticed, though, about fashion or any creative process—it never lets you rest. You always see something that gives you ideas that percolate. It's a blessing and a curse. I would go to Europe twice a year alone, traveling to six countries in four days. It was exhausting, but I always came back with concepts for the next season's line.

So, it was no different in Aspen. I got an idea there that became one of the most successful knitted fabrics ever made. On a ski lift, I was in a chair behind a young lady who was wearing real denim patchwork.

As a matter of fact, I followed this woman for the rest of the day, looking at her denim with stars in my eyes. I realized this was a design I thought I could sell to the only major manufacturer I had never sold anything to: Levi Strauss & Co. When I got back to New York, we started to refine the ideas and patterns. I thought we had a real winner.

The specs were different shades of denim patches in shapes of boxes of all different sizes, no one less than three inches but it could go up to six inches, sewn together to make one fabric. Because of our computer knitting machines, each yard would be different, and therefore, no garment would be the same.

This had never been done before—a patterned fabric with no repeat. You couldn't even do this with printed fabrics. I did make some changes with the stitching, and the designing team did a great job. The beauty of it was we had no additional cost to make it; nobody knew that. We could also make this on all our machines, overnight.

No one else in the industry could do this. Angelo made me a suit from the new fabric. (I was still using Angelo as my tailor, and the store took pride in my success. I guess I was always somewhat superstitious.) I started to advertise the Brooke Industries' advantages. We had the largest 100-percent computerized mill in the industry, yet we were one of the smallest plants out there. No one else had 100-percent computerized machines, though. So, it was true, but perhaps a little misleading.

Demand went way up, and I was a genius (maybe). Levi Strauss did buy the fabric, but they wanted an exclusive. I gave it to them, but it was a big mistake—they didn't buy enough fabric to warrant an exclusive deal. My ego got the better of me there. In any case, they were not successful with it. They continued to buy other fabrics from us, so I think it wasn't a total failure.

One of my salesmen suggested that we should sell it to womenswear. After all, he argued, that's how you first saw it used in Aspen. In womenswear, they bought all the time and, in some cases, even before they made a sample.

Machines started running the patchwork. That was the start, and this went on for months. And then a year. It became seven days a week, twenty-four hours a day running the same denim design.

No one else could run this type of production, I thought. Well, I was very wrong. Six months later, some competing mills shut down their production for weeks, reprogramming their machines to make patchwork denim.

This was difficult to do on their noncomputerized machines,

requiring the changing of thousands of knitting needles per machine, multiplied by hundreds of machines. By hand. It was a huge project.

In contrast, all we had to do was place a pattern on a reel-to-reel tape and push a button. So, you can imagine how in-demand this fabric was for our competitors to go through these time-consuming and expensive changes. It was surely worth their efforts, though.

Years later, I met someone at a cocktail party at his magnificent house on the water in the Hamptons. When he discovered that I created the patchwork denim, he said, "Thank you, Jerry. See the house you are standing in? That fabric paid for it."

## The Inevitable Union

At this point, the Lodi mill was becoming a burden. I caught one of the men on the night shift stealing. I saw him on one of our security cameras and fired him. That was not enough to stop him from going to the union. That's when I found out about what great power the unions carry.

Until then, I had only known about unions from my parents. My father had worked for the International Ladies' Garment Workers' Union (ILGWU) his whole accounting career, and my mother started working for them after my brother and I went off to school on our own. They were staunch allies. Now I saw the union from the other side, and it was not pretty.

First, I got a call from Mr. Green. He was a union organizer. He said that the union was going to strike against us if we did not enter a contract with them. That meant they would take a vote of the workers, including the one I fired. Then, according to Mr. Green, the mill would certainly become a union shop. I reviewed the legalities and found out I couldn't stop them.

With Mark now gone and the onus of union recognition hanging over me at the Lodi facility, it was easy to decide that I didn't need or want to own and operate my own mill any longer. It was fine when Mark was operating it, and it was running smoothly, but now it was about to become a big burden for me.

I had to get out from under it all before it buried me completely. And besides, the Lodi mill was generating only about 20 percent of our entire production—and the rest was being produced very efficiently and profitably at the contract mills we had relationships with down south. Time to plan our getaway.

We made an agreement with one of the southern mills we did business with to take over the Lodi production. I'd be able to close the doors, and not miss a year's worth of knit production to boot.

Making the move south presented a real problem with the union, and the Lodi mill was dead in their crosshairs. My plan was—in its simple form—to take the yarns and other valuable materials that would be required to continue production down south and load up some trucks and send them on their way down to their new home.

It surely wasn't going to be that easy. If the union found out about the move and its motives, they would have followed my trucks and then strike that southern mill. That would have been entirely legal, but not good for anyone.

Businesses in the south were not unionized, and the implications of all this was complicated and sure to be unpleasant.

Besides, it probably would have changed the friendly demeanor of my southern associates, and not for the better. It was time for a little ingenuity, intrigue, and covert maneuvers.

The union had picketers in front of the mill and we agreed to close for just one day (to fix a phony electrical problem). Everyone heard, and my master plan moved along. My plant manager sympathetically agreed that it would be best to do it on a Sunday. I agreed.

Conveniently, there were only two male strikers in the driveway on Sundays. (The whole thing was a great improvisation ensemble performance, in hindsight.) Our mill was in a residential neighborhood in Lodi. Before trucks started to show up, I hired two good-looking ladies from 42nd Street to distract the two picketers. They were both gone before we knew it. I was beginning to feel a little like James Bond.

Now the shell game had begun. All I needed was four trailers to take the yarn; I hired six. The two extras were decoys. When the distracted picketing men left the mill, I brought in the trucks and parked them in the back of the building. Later that Sunday, the trucks started to make a move. The first truck picked up only waste; the second took yarn.

I followed the first and had one of my designers follow the second. When I was sure they weren't being followed, I called the other trucks and told them their final destination. The yarn and other materials arrived on time. The Lodi mill was now empty. I was very relieved. I know there must have been an easier way to do it, but looking back, it was exciting and a lot of fun, if not a good story to tell.

Meanwhile, in a perfect dangerous storm of a rapidly changing marketplace, knits began to get a bad reputation because of all the inferior fabric that reached the stores. All these mercenary garage operators with one or two machines simply didn't know what they were doing.

To save money, they used yarns improperly that were guaranteed to result in lousy fabrics—and therefore equally lousy garments. Never a good situation for extended sales. For a quick background of how these amateurs operated, they used yarns that were 100-percent polyester textured, instead of 100-percent textured polyester. The names were similar but the difference in quality was night and day. And so was the price.

To make more money, they greedily bought cheap material. The finished product made with the inferior yarns looked very similar to fabric produced with the expensive yarns, even for the knowledgeable buyers. But their fabric would pill, snag, and stretch easily. It was a horrible product.

They killed the market right before our eyes, and there was nothing we could do to stop it. The toothpaste was out of the tube, as they say. It became a joke how bad it had become because of these opportunists. Johnny Carson even started to make jokes about polyester knits—and he had helped start the craze. It was all ending right before my eyes.

To make matters worse, they kept coming out with new designs—horrible designs, produced with the inferior fabrics. It was embarrassing. These talentless copycats bastardized what we had done to have men finally dress casually and individually in a bona-fide shift of a huge cultural paradigm.

At that time, changing from the dark suit uniforms and ties to the freedom to celebrate individuality was the main driving force. I became sorry for what I had started. To this day, I feel as though I live in the shadow of this trend and what it devolved into in the fabric and apparel business.

The truth is the knitting industry was in its infancy. New technology and advances would lead to where you wouldn't have been able to tell the difference between a woven fabric or a knit, except the knit would be more comfortable, last longer, and be less expensive. In the end, it was capitalism at its worst. People who didn't know what they were doing destroyed the advancement of the textiles and gave me a bad name for having started it

The big mills took back control with their woven goods. I tried to make woven goods with one of the finest mills in New England. These woven goods were a total disaster. It seems that my quality control man inspected the fabric before the final step in finishing. This step gave the goods an incredibly silky feel. We sold their total production, and everyone was happy until the problem began.

The final finishing process pressed the fabric so smoothly that you could accidently slip your fingers through it. The manufacturer didn't realize this until they made their garments. It was a dire situation.

We tried to salvage some of the garments, like placing the pants in a vat with a strengthening agent to make the material strong. The problem was you had to put in so much agent that the pants could almost stand by themselves. It might have been comical if it wasn't my business.

One customer described a complaint he got: "At a wedding,

his crotch simply fell out. And he was the best man."

Knits were going out of favor anyway, and I just ruined half of my customers with this bad fabric. The future was bleak. I had stayed in business for too long. An important skill is knowing when to get off the train and I clearly missed my stop. The market shrank, so did the competition; we were one of the last to survive. But finally, we had to close Brooke Industries. It was a mostly good five-year run, but it was clearly over.

The leisure suit changed how men dressed forever, it took them out of the box and put them into fashion, and it became an accepted and individualistic freedom with casual dress. I had my first taste of success and craved more.

# Legal Lofts NYC ③
## Lawless Manhattan Living

**1977**

New York City is plunged into darkness because of a blackout. Thousands are stranded and looting, and mayhem ensues. Peanut farmer Jimmy Carter is elected president. Elvis Presley dies at forty-two. *Star Wars* and *Roots* are released. Apple releases the Apple II computer. India Prime Minister Indira Gandhi resigns from office. Abe Beam is the mayor of NYC. City living is at its grittiest.

Here I was, married, with two children to support, no job, and a mortgage to pay. I had spent ten years in the profitable textile business when Japanese imports began taking all our business away. I realized that this was a turning point, and although I put in all the energy I could to sustain Brooke Industries, I knew it was time to say goodbye. I had to find a new concept.

It was time for a change, and I knew that. The only minor issue that I faced was that I had no experience in anything other than textiles. I decided to try to create a business with no employees at all. It stemmed from the guilt I felt when I was forced to close Brooke Industries and my employees lost their jobs. Most had been with me for over six years and had become friends. I knew they had families to support, and I felt like I had failed them.

I remember how much I hated calling them into my extravagant offices. What were they thinking? I didn't want to go through that again; I wanted a one-man show. Look, it's me. I'm a man. So, I explored.

I checked my checklist: Boar's Head meat routes, laundromats, car wash, arcades, pizza parlors, etc. I believed nearly all of these were fronts and had some involvement with the mob, or at least that's what I heard.

I wanted my brother's opinion on all this and, thinking back, wanted to do something with someone I could trust, rely on, and share success with. We loved each other, even though we were like oil and water. I was water; then we switched places. It worked; we were close, thick as thieves they say.

I moved to the suburbs; he moved to the suburbs. I got married; he got married. He became a very successful lawyer, establishing his own immigration practice, Howard Rosengarten, LLC. I just had ideas. We always believed we should work together.

Howard was very instrumental in offering me the financial life raft I desperately needed emotionally. After all, I had a family. Perhaps he was able to do so because he had a propensity to buy cheap, and I was inexpensive.

His decision-making was based on cost and cost alone. I, on the other hand, have a very different perspective on this. I have a much higher tolerance for risk. (I really believe the higher the risk, the higher the reward.) I am not sure what he was so stressed about; in our over forty years of working together, he always had financial safety from his law practice.

What skills, other than my strong sense of style, could I use? Surely knowing clothing was not the ONLY field I mastered over the previous ten years. Finally, it came to me: real estate. I had rented offices, built a mill, and bought a house in Plandome, a village in Long Island.

## Real Estate.

It was 1978, and our timing couldn't have been better. NYC was going bankrupt, and a new mayor was boldly taking the horse by the reins. Ed Koch knew what he was getting into. New York City was a disaster. The place was filthy, crime ran rampant, and all the successful businesses were moving out. People were angry. We were praying for someone like Koch and hoped he would be able to end this chaos and put a stop to the city's dreadful downward spiral. NYC real estate was in the dumps. I turned my sights on opportunities there.

Koch had a charismatic quality and was a true cheerleader for our city, but the problem took a while to correct. Factory buildings in SoHo were going vacant. I saw promise in the concept of converting these buildings to residential use. I had sold my house for twice as much as I bought for it. So why not here in the city of New York?

I didn't know what it took to do this—I had no experience in construction—but the potential seemed clear to me. If I sold 16 homes in a building, it would be another hit. If I bought the right building at the right price, I would have a new business.

Step one: find a place.

I consider what happened next one of my finer rides.

With Howard's help, I began my search for a vacant factory building in local newspapers, where the city's auctions were announced.

I nearly killed myself while doing a "walk-through" during the first building I went to see. It was a brick building about seven stories high at 20th Street and 2nd Avenue in Manhattan. It was institutional-looking and had solid bones. Before entering, I was required to sign a liability release. Just in case. The city really had no clue, nor did they care, of the dangerous conditions inside.

I breezed through the first, then second and third floors, and finally, I made my way into the basement. I always knew to check the foundations. There were many doors down there, all for the utility rooms of the building. At first glance, the floor seemed to be made of cement, the same color as the rest of the basement. So, I did not hesitate to open the door and take a step inside.

This room turned out to be the elevator pit, and I tumbled right into it, face down! It was filled with about four feet of disgusting water, which broke my fall. There I was, drenched in the middle of winter; if I hadn't died from embarrassment, I would likely have died from pneumonia.

I felt like I was an idiot to sign the liability release. But even more of an idiot knowing that I could have owned that building for nothing if I truly hurt myself. I never told anyone about this incident, not even my brother. (He would use it against me, I'm sure. You know how older brothers are.)

The other city buildings I visited were mainly on the lower east side of Alphabet City, Avenue A to Avenue C. No one could, or even wanted to, maintain these old sites. The city officials were clearly avoiding that headache. What I saw in these buildings was out of the scenes of a horror movie. I was in complete and utter shock.

"How can anyone, even squatters, live here?" I thought.

Spread throughout the floor were huge gaps, leaving large sink holes for anyone (or anything) to dive into. The ceilings were crumbling, and the walls, made up of just some plaster, were plunging down. They were neglected for over twenty-five years, except by the homeless.

These were old brownstones built in the twenties. If they were located on any avenues toward the west, they would have been worth a fortune, even back then. The squalor went on for blocks. People were squatting in these buildings without heat or running water. You wouldn't believe this was America, especially New York City.

I remember one particularly egregious building. I signed another waiver and proceeded with caution. The first floor was closed. You could only get in using the ladder from the fire escape located on the second floor. Although these civil servants had no nerve, they knew they could count on hungry developers to literally "step up." I climbed in; hey, if this was what it took to be a successful developer, I was game.

It was worse than I could have imagined. Not only were there gaping holes in the ground, but there were also missing floors altogether. Some levels were without a ceiling entirely. In fact, you could see the sky from any place on the second floor.

Within five minutes, I had seen enough. The second floor could not hold the number of people coming in. I had a flashback to my little swim in the first building, and I wanted out. I pushed my way toward the window, through the incoming crowd, and made it out to the fire escape. That's where I saw an unexpected sight. The blocks were full of picketers waving signs.

DON'T KICK US OUT OF OUR HOMES.

DEATH TO DEVELOPERS.

WE DON'T WANT YOU HERE.

GO HOME.

I swore off going to another city auction, no matter what my brother said. That's when I made a career decision: I would never buy an occupied building, especially with rent control tenants. Most people don't know the origin story so let me explain.

After World War II, there was a housing shortage. So, the city came up with "rent stabilization," and millions signed on. Why wouldn't they? They were given apartments where landlords couldn't increase rents unless the city and state government gave an increase and that rarely happened.

So, the only reason to buy one of those buildings was that the people would eventually die. That would free up the apartment to fair market rent. But the city then said that any family member could take over one of these apartments. That is why they have lasted generations.

## Loft-Living Before It Was Hip

The idea of developing legal lofts came from a tour that I took with a woman named Selena Gadot. She ran a tour of artist lofts in SoHo that intrigued me. They were working studios and totally illegal for use as living quarters.

Landlords lost their industrial tenants; these companies moved south and left NYC. They wanted to build their facilities on larger plots with local tax relief, financial aid, and new workforce. They also preferred to get as far away as they could from the unions.

In their wake stood abandoned factory buildings, mostly in the SoHo, Chelsea, and Meatpacking areas of Manhattan. In those days, lofts had yet to become popular. People didn't understand this style or type of living, and they were against code. That is until it became fiercely attractive.

I'm not sure how or when it happened, but I started to see artists take over these empty spaces. I was lucky to get into real estate before Ed Koch took office, he was the new Mayor and turned the city around, which made most buildings unaffordable to me. Prices were low, and I could ride the wave. I was able to sign two contracts for industrial buildings. One was on 23rd Street and the other on 4th Ave.

At first, they were tenants, just like the manufacturers. Artists would take over an entire floor, clean it out and enhance their new, open space with new doors, walls, kitchens, and bathrooms. Some were more well-off artists, and they got creative with their renovations.

One that particularly stood out had twenty-foot ceilings, windows on all four sides, with beautiful mahogany wooden floors.

It made sense; artists needed the considerable room, the abundance of light, and, of course, the low rent. Imagine, you could get a 5,000-10,000-square-foot loft for around $800 a month.

It is important to note that these new tenants and not-so-new landlords were completely breaking code. It is illegal to allow residency in a commercial space. But this was an unusual time.

Like most government agencies, when (and only when) they choose to, they turn a blind eye. How else were they going to get out of the economic crisis? The city's tax base depended on these rental transactions. As did the landlords.

Those who wanted to stay in the city saw the trend and living in a loft became special. I saw the demand and acted on my gut. If I could create loft spaces within factory buildings and make them proper legal residences, it would be a home run. No one had done this, legally that is, and I was ready, willing, and able.

Now I was in contract to buy those buildings I mentioned. Despite my promise never to go to another auction, I found myself standing with Howard at another one. I had received a notice for the sell-off of The Induction Center. The title of the venue was enough to catch my attention. This was the armed forces center for enlistment during the Vietnam War. It was a different type of auction, though, held and organized by the U.S. Army. This opportunity could change both my life and Howard's life forever.

This high rise was perched in the middle of the Financial District-Wall Street area. She sat on Whitehall Street adjacent to the Hudson River, and it occupied a whole block, not a big block, but big enough for me.

The floor plan showed that it was about 20,000 square feet

with windows on all sides. It had the most magnificent open atrium in the center and antique rod iron elevators from the '20s. The railings, also rod iron, stretched around the perimeter, creating walkways off every office or apartment.

I had seen this building before under very different circumstances, but that didn't stop me from looking. I had been much younger, and the United States Armed Services had called me in for a medical examination. They wanted to draft me to serve in the army. It was the first test I was delighted to fail—my feet were too flat.

I distinctly remember this building seeming so ominous at the time. The elevators were old, not grand like the ones I had mentioned, and the light green color of the walls was barely a color at all, more like a whitewash. It was a traumatic experience, one that I will never forget.

Now, I wanted to own this building. But I was getting a little ahead of myself. I was in the midst of construction building my first loft building. I think I was going through my manic phase. I saw the endless design possibilities of using the existing building. I'm sure others would have taken it down and built a new one from scratch.

I wanted to have an impressive project and preserve history. It was a great spot, no matter what its origin. I was constructing my first loft building and had eyes to grow as fast as I could. As I said: manic. So, this was a great opportunity.

The army had strict guidelines for putting in bids. The auction was held in person at the site, not like the others I was used to. Your offer had to be on a specific date and at 4:00 p.m. on the dot. After that time, they would accept no more bids.

I needed my architect to look at the Army Induction Center and tell me if I could build what I wanted. I made him promise not to share the news of the auction with any other clients.

We met, and my instincts were right. He loved it. I went back to my site and discussed the new project with my brother. He got excited, even though we both didn't really know much about what the construction would cost.

Step two: find the funds.

I needed to find the money. How much? I had no idea.

As it so happens, being in the right place at the right time was the gift of good luck I was handed, yet again. A young kid in my architect's office had once approached me, mentioning how his father was looking to invest in Manhattan real estate. He had over-heard me talking to my architect about this building and wanted the chance to be involved together with his dad. I said that was okay, and we set up a meeting between the kid, his father, Burt, and me.

We met at the Regency Hotel and made a deal then and there. I guess I had been given a good recommendation. Burt would finance the deal, and he would come up with all the seed money. I would renovate the building. We would each own 50 percent of the asset.

This train was leaving the station. The night before the auc-tion, there was a severe snowstorm, the worst the city had seen in years. My brother and I decided to come in from the suburbs and spend the night in the city.

We were at Whitehall at 3:45 p.m. the following day. The room was nearly empty, maybe four other bidders. As the clock struck 4:00 p.m., one of three officers in full uniform announced, "The bidding is officially closed." All hell broke loose.

Five men burst through the door. The one who seemed like the leader was shouting at the top of his lungs, "I have a bid!"

"No!" I roared. "The bidding has already been closed. He's too late."

I stared at the officials and said, "You set the rules, and rules are rules, especially when they come from the army."

I was winning the argument. The crowd seemed to agree with me.

Then, the late bidder yelled one word as loud as he could, "SNOW!"

For just this moment, everyone and everything froze. The pause was short, and quickly we all got back to business. The officers huddled together for a moment, and when they reemerged, they accepted his offer over mine. No matter what we said, no matter what we did, my group came in second place. It might as well have been last. We lost. I was devastated.

It turns out that this winner was a very close client of my architect. My partner's son was in his office when he got the call from the winner. He overheard them congratulating each other. I realized that my competitor was the first person my architect called after I took him to see the location.

I was seething with anger and wanted revenge. My brother once advised me not to go after anyone at the time of the evil deed. Instead, wait until he is not expecting it, catch him off guard, and it will be that much more effective. So, although I was at the breaking point, I took his advice. Also, he was in the middle of approving my other project, so it was probably not the best time.

The Department of Buildings, like most municipalities, implemented tedious systems to get things done. You needed a certified architect to draw plans and submit them to the correct division to be certified by the city.

New York City, however, had its own variation, and an architect certified in New York could approve and sign off on their own work without any inspection or approvals. The city protected itself by doing random checks on these self-certifications. Many architects lost their licenses because of this process. I still had to get the plumbing and electric sign-off. I had to bite my lip for a couple of months.

The building was a seven-story structure of about 32,000 square feet. The man who owned it said it was part of an estate, and as it turned out, it was his estate. I still don't know why he kept that a secret. We went round and round on price, but I knew I would get him down to my price. No one was buying anything in New York. After all, the city was going under. What I needed was a long closing and a small down payment on the contract.

He eventually agreed, and I had my first project.

The building was old, but it had some unique qualities—a huge elevator, two fire escapes, one in the front and one in the back, and two courtyards on the east and west sides.

This building used to be storage for Macy's as a warehouse. They filled every floor with all the items they used for the Thanksgiving Day Parade and display fixtures for their windows. All this stuff had seen better days but was usable for someone. It would take months to empty everything.

After I had received a bunch of quotes that were too high

from demolition companies, I had an idea. I went to a store called Anne's Plastic and told them I was emptying a storage warehouse filled with the display items from Macy's. They got very excited, so I told them they could have the whole building exclusively if they paid me $1,000 a floor, and they had to start at the top floor and work their way down.

They agreed, and I had taken care of that problem, except as I watched them after two weeks, I could see they were slowing down. They quit after five floors. They just couldn't take any more. I finished emptying the balance with one of those demolition companies.

Now I had 32,000 square feet of clean open space and was ready for my lofts to be created. I had seven full floors and one half a floor on the roof. The problem with most spaces like this was that they were cavernous open spaces with windows in the front and back of the building. A room, in legal terms, must have light and air (windows).

That meant that the only living space was in the front or back of the building. This space had two courtyards, which gave me legal requirements for light and air. It would make these lofts much more flexible. I divided the floors in half. Each unit needed two means of egress, which I had already in place. (Remember those fire escapes.)

To make a space livable and get a C.O. (Certificate of Occupancy), you needed two things: a bathroom and a kitchen. That was my next challenge. I couldn't afford to put in fifteen of them.

So, I went to every cabinetmaker in the area and found one whose work I liked. I explained to the owner the job scope but confessed I couldn't afford to pay him.

We made a deal. I would pay for it, and he would put in two model units. The balance would be paid for by the purchasers, and at the end of the job, I would pay for the models at cost. At cost is a funny term. It could cost you anyone's cost. You must be careful with your negotiations. I could have asked for a commission, but I felt that would be pushing it.

I had no money. I had spent just about everything on the purchase of the building. I was going to sell these lofts, so I went to my factor (you know, the loan sharks in textiles that I had done business with). This was a far cry from the textiles, but he was a friend, and I guess he had confidence in me. When I closed Brooke Industries, I took care of all my payables, including his.

My life lesson is never to burn bridges. He agreed to help and gave me a loan for 50 percent of my projected sales. That gave me breathing room and enabled me to complete construction on this building and purchase the next property.

I knew I was out of my depth but hanging on. I treated this building as a new line of fabrics. Except this time, there were renderings of the building's kitchens, baths, and floor plan in my brochure. A customer could see exactly what I was selling. You had to produce a prospectus, which was a legal document approved by the attorney general if you wanted to make a co-op or condominium.

I decided to make this building a co-op. I did this because I could offer lower prices to the buyers. With a co-op, you're selling shares in a company, not actual real estate. The buyers needed less cash because the mortgage was never considered.

This really is a sleight of hand, but everyone knew it. Then, I set up shop. My office consisted of a desk and a phone in this vacant building. Just me and a phone. As with all these projects, there is a waiting game to find that first buyer. Once the engine starts, though it's like a runaway train. You must hold on for dear life.

I oversaw every bit of the construction from the flooring and walls to the electricity and plumbing. I put windows through brick walls so residents would be able to enjoy each of the courtyards. I designed two models, one being an open floor plan loft-style, and the other with bedrooms (a hybrid loft plus standard apartment).

My first tenant was a gay couple who made an offer after just the first visit. I hadn't finished either sample unit when they appeared. They had requested that their unit remain completely unfinished, and I agreed. I had a good feeling about them, and I was right. They designed a spectacular unit, which was exactly what I needed. They allowed me to use it as a model loft that enabled me to sell the rest of the building.

Now I get to the hard part. I had to pressure the buyers to close on these units to wrap up and close on the next building I was purchasing. That meant I had to have, in hand, the C.O. of all the units, which were supposedly fully done. My skills from back in the textile world kicked in.

Back then, I was always under the gun to get my line out. I would work in the mill until 4:00 a.m. to design my line. The pressure was equally as demanding when getting the final C.O. I worked weekends and nights and was almost at the finish line.

The only holdup was a little yellow card handed over by Con Ed, the utility company. They were notorious for dragging out their responsibilities in loft buildings. I went down to Con Ed's main office to finally get an inspection of the building. I had to beg the clerk (that wouldn't be the last time either, I became quite good at it). Acting 101 improvs worked!

The inspector came, and the situation went from intense to crushing pressure. The gas lines had to be tested. These lines were behind walls intertwined with other building plumbing systems. I had never seen this kind of test before, and I wasn't ready for bad results, which could add months to the C.O.

The test itself is quite simple; they pump air in the gas lines under pressure overnight. The next day they read the meter to see if it has lost any pressure, which indicates a leak but not where it's coming from. Luckily, the pressure held.

No more hiccups. I was able to close on my next loft building. She was a beauty, different from any building I was ever in or ever saw. Her size alone was most unusual. While many of the buildings in Greenwich Village were about twenty-five or fifty feet wide by one-hundred feet deep, this vision was twenty-five feet wide by 175-feet deep. It was shaped like a rifle.

When I brought my architect and accountant to the site, they outright rejected my plans. So, I had to replace them. They couldn't visualize what I could see. To them, everything was black or white, and this was not the first time we had disagreed.

This also wasn't the first time that my mind envisioned the potential of the things I was looking at. No one really saw what I saw. It was a challenging, perplexing project, one that I wanted to do. It was a risk but well worth it if I was right.

Let me try and give you some detail about this alluring design and why I needed to have it. She was so long and narrow and had other critical features that more than added to her value. When you entered the building, you walked sixty feet to the elevator. So, if you wanted two units on a floor, you had a lot of wasted area. But the space would be fantastic.

You see, something I had learned over those years was that when a structure is narrow and long, in many cases, they give off far more light and air than others. This building had a hundred feet of windows on both the eastern and northern exposure. You could sit and enjoy your morning coffee in one spot in a room, and if you turned your head in one direction, you could stare at the World Trade Center. Turn toward another direction, and you could gaze at the Empire State Building.

The hall length of over seventy feet was concerning from a design standpoint because of unusable space; there was also a sound issue. The longer the wall, the more of a problem you have.

I decided to divide the lofts with a front and rear unit, creating the most space possible. That meant a very long hallway before you even stepped foot into the apartment. Always solution orientated, I morphed this space into a private art gallery for the owner. They loved the idea.

Most apartments in conventional buildings share maybe fifteen feet of adjoining space. Here we had over a hundred feet, and you could hear EVERYTHING. I could foresee the lawsuits and complaints already. My customer was concerned about how he would get his grand piano into the loft.

"It's no problem," I assured him. "Let me get back to you."

By the way, "It's not a problem" is my reflex quote. You will hear it over and over.

I learned about sound and the fact that it's carried through space using vibrations. If you eliminate vibration, you eliminate sound. And that's what I did. It was a tactic that would, and still does, come in handy, as you'll see.

To eliminate the flow of vibrational sound, build two walls. Use very narrow studs and tracks and cut the top layer of the floor or put rubber on each track. That's it! The face of each wall muffles the sound, and the one-inch space kills the vibration: therefore, no noise. Mission accomplished!

This theory was proven well to me when one of the owners was making a movie inside the front loft. I was in the back unit, and I swear to this day that I did not hear anything. I went around to the front because I was curious to see the set. There were empty pizza boxes and lighting equipment all over the hallway. I slowly pushed the door open and peeked through the crack.

I stood there, paralyzed for a second while I was determining what to do next. Someone must have noticed me. Was I staring?

They shouted, "What do you want?!?"

I remembered to breathe and finally asked for "A slice of pizza, please."

They were filming an X-rated movie! It was quite a scene, to say the least. There must have been at least ten men in the crew, directing, producing, guiding, and supervising. There was a hot tub and two actors, or so I thought. Later, I found out many of the crew had roles as well. And I was worried about the noise coming out of the grand piano?! Eating pizza has never been the same since.

● ● ●

I decided it was time for me to have a real office. It was inconvenient doing business while traveling from site to site. The first floor of the building at 59 4th Avenue seemed just right. It was nothing like the MGM building, yet it gave the feeling of the factory offices that my customers had during my textile days.

Located in the back half of the first floor, it was a no-brainer. The ceiling heights were higher than the rest of the building, about fourteen feet. It was a big open space with very little natural light. One antique wall was made of glass panes about five by seven inches, and it had a walkway in the middle.

The front of the building was a shoe store, Pappagallo Outlet, which ended up being one of the side ventures my brother and I got involved in along the way.

It could have been a challenge to sell these lofts if the buyers didn't see my vision. I was lucky they did. The buyers I had in mind were an exciting group that included architects, accountants, artists, computer wizards, and one nice lady interested in the lower-level back unit. She wanted it brought back to its original state.

"That's no problem," I affirmed.

Then I had to find out how I could make it happen and who would get this done.

It was a lot harder than I had imagined. Everyone I spoke to knew the "how" part, but no one agreed they actually would do the work. They just didn't want to take the risk.

I tried to convince her to allow me to simply make the space look and feel like it had originally. She would not hear of it but solved that problem by buying the entire floor. I had to sell it to her because I liked her.

Next, I went out to find an Italian artisan to re-create the original. The tailor from my past, Angelo, told me he had a cousin who had just arrived in the States and was looking for work. He ended up working for me for more than ten years. Never burn your bridges.

The building looked like an old factory from the outside. I didn't have to make the entrance look special like they do today. The crime rate in the city was out of control; none of the tenants in the building wanted to attract the attention of outsiders to their expensive lofts.

The Pappagallo Shoe Outlet occupied both the first and the second floors. They were a well-known brand name of expensive women's shoes, and this was their only outlet store. I knew nothing about shoes other than the fact that women loved them.

The business owners were ready to retire, and their children had no desire to take over the family business. They had two years left on their lease and wanted out of that obligation. I let them out of the lease but had a bigger play in mind.

I wanted to take over the business, and that is exactly what we did. This purchase was not so much a financial risk but a piece of the puzzle. If I wanted the second floor to sell, I would have to free up the space. We brought in a friend as a partner to run the shoe store. Later, we found out he had a shoe or foot fetish, which became a liability. Anyway, this business didn't last long because the parent company did not want this outlet at all. We worked out a buyout of the lease.

The units in the front part of the second floor were most problematic. They just didn't sell like the others. Although not built out yet, all the upper floors were completely sold. Each unit was the owner's design, and they constructed what they wanted at their own expense. If they preferred, I would build them at their cost, under a different contract.

One day this heavyset man walked to my office and asked to talk to me. I never asked how he heard of me. Joel was his name, and he had a meek voice. He was from a very wealthy family from Texas; most people would recognize the name. I didn't know it until a friend told me.

On his first visit, he bought the front unit on the second floor. I explained the property line problem and that another building could block all his windows except the front, but he didn't seem to care. Also, he was paying all cash, no mortgage. This was unheard of. At that time, everyone had to use the bank to make a purchase. You didn't know if you had a sale until the bank approved.

The building was now fully occupied, and I was happy as hell. Until one evening when I received a strange phone call. I was informed that the tenant on the second floor was bringing in young boys at very late hours, and it looked suspicious. Since I was the one who had sold the space to him, it was my obligation to investigate and make sure everything was kosher.

I confronted Joel the next day, explaining the serious accusations against him. As it turned out, he had set up a foundation for underprivileged youth, mentoring them and providing funding for their education. I checked it out and was relieved that what he disclosed appeared to be the truth. I reported my results to the board.

However, six months later, I read a front-page story in the *Post* detailing what Joel was doing. His family name did not help hide this story; he was in all the papers. He was convicted of pedo-philia and sentenced to about twenty years. I guess that's why he didn't care about the windows being blocked; as a matter of fact, for him, it was a plus.

I felt weirdly responsible for these young kids, even though I knew I wasn't. The other tenants also seemed to blame me for this horrible occurrence. He seemed so nice, like someone who couldn't hurt a fly. It just goes to show how looks can be deceiving.

I came back after a two-week vacation and began looking for my next project. The market had accelerated like a rocket. The prices of loft buildings had risen to the point that I had to drop out as a buyer. I couldn't compete in the market; it was too risky even for me.

Additionally, it became even more difficult because of the IMD law, which gave all loft tenants the same rights as rent-stabilized tenants. This changed the ability to negotiate with tenants and building owners. This was done to correct a problem that the city ignored for years. It's that simple. They sign a piece of paper, and it's a new law.

How was I to buy a building without the money to do so? Now I had to get creative. It was time to change tracks.

# The Restaurateur
## The Best Thing I Ever Ate

### 1980/2009

John Lennon is shot and killed in front of his residence at the Dakota building. Rubik's Cube becomes a huge fad. Iran-Iraq war begins. CNN begins its first live broadcasting. 3M launches Post-it Notes. There is a severe heat wave sweeping the United States. The USA hockey team defeats the Soviet Union in "The Miracle on Ice." Let's eat!

Restaurants have played important roles in my life throughout my career. In the neighborhoods where I had active projects, I would seek out local places and find ones where I felt at home and visit them often. You can get a real family feeling being a regular in a neighborhood restaurant, and I've met some wonderful people this way.

## Cooper Square Café (1980)

In 1980, I was converting my second loft building in the Village on 4th Avenue and 9th Street. As was my usual pattern, I found a special restaurant for my daily lunch. It was on the corner just next to my project and was very convenient to get to.

In a short time, I became friendly with Tony, the owner. Soon, we began eating together on an almost daily basis. We waited for his rush times to end so we could dine more casually.

Tony was a short, heavyset Italian man in his mid-fifties and always wore the same apron, covered in stains. It always looked like the same apron to me, at least.

Tony's place was a typical neighborhood "greasy-spoon" coffee shop. You really did need to check your utensils before you ate. Like a lot of similar joints, the food was basic but good and I felt right at home there.

Tony and I would talk for hours as our friendship grew. He began complaining about falling behind on his mortgage payments and not being able to make ends meet. He owned the building the restaurant was in, a one-story structure.

Our conversations went on for months while I was building out my project at 59 4th Avenue. Eventually, Tony asked me for help in the form of a loan. And he kept asking. Each time, I told him that it was not my business to lend money. I've always said that if you lend money to a friend, you end up losing both your money and the friend (not very original).

Eventually, I said I would help him out by buying the building—that was my business. So, I bought the building and became Tony's landlord with a promise to clean up the coffee shop. He was relieved and happy to be out from under the pressure of it all.

The place needed a lot of work. Everything was falling apart. So, I set out to redesign and remodel the entire place while making sure to keep it as a coffee shop. As soon as we closed on the property, I demolished everything and began reworking it.

It wasn't a big project, but I found it interesting to be applying my creativity to a restaurant—something I had never done before. I insisted on keeping the menu almost exactly as it was so we wouldn't lose Tony's established customers. After all, I wanted the rent to get paid since I was now the landlord.

Just as everything was nearly set and we were getting ready to reopen, I was walking in the neighborhood, and I saw some heavy equipment being delivered to a large storefront just a few blocks away that had been vacant for years.

I asked one of the workmen, "What's going in here?"

He said they were setting up a large coffee shop. This delivery was their baking ovens, and he noted that they would be making everything on-premises. My instincts sharpened and my heart dropped. I saw my investment going down the drain, killed by a sharp competitor with better food.

I called Tony and told him what I had just seen and heard. I could tell that he was very concerned. Just like me. But you can always have a better restaurant, I said, so "Let's up our game." He quickly said, "Yes, I'm Italian, and I can cook like one." Well, that was enough for me. My wife is Italian, and good cucina Italiano has a special place in my world. I was going into the fine dining business!

It was time to get serious. Once I'm on the scent of a project, I go all in. I stopped the construction on the coffee shop and recalculated what I was doing. I doubled the budget and designed a new space fit for a fine restaurant. When it was finished, it was beautiful. (This was well before the noted Union Square Café came to the area.)

I had no restaurant experience except for a brief stint as a bumbling, dyslexic waiter who made a lot of friends mostly by the power of personality. I was ready to be a restaurateur, though, and really felt good about the opportunity that had somehow appeared in front of me. I knew that I couldn't trust Tony to create a menu, hire the waitstaff, and do everything else that was necessary to bring a successful dining spot to life, so I took it all on. I just can't help myself. Living on the edge of the unknown is exhilarating to me.

I needed someone to help guide me to create a menu for a fine restaurant like I wanted the Cooper Square Café to become. I really didn't know anyone who knew how to cook, and then I remembered Naomi. I met Naomi when I was out of work after I left the textile business. One of my partners tried to find me opportunities, and he suggested I look at a company called Montana Palace. Life is a funny puzzle. If you really look, you can put all the pieces together.

Montana Palace was a one-woman operation making and selling prepared foods, and Naomi was that woman. Her cooking was wonderful and delicious, and she was a remarkable force of nature. I learned that Naomi had once been married to a rabbi and was now living and working in a storefront with her two daughters.

She told me how difficult it was being married to an orthodox rabbi, and she didn't want her girls to go through that. So, she left her husband without a penny in her pocket and went back to what she knew and started making and selling amazing, people-pleasing prepared foods.

At the time, some of the best food stores in Manhattan were carrying her foods. One of the best, Balducci's, couldn't get enough to satisfy the demand. Naomi's cheesecakes—espresso, dark chocolate, Kahlua, and even limoncello—were especially heavenly, and I would have made an investment in her business after the first taste of her desserts.

I called and set up a preliminary meeting with Naomi. We talked for a while and discussed the restaurant business. As usual, I started to explore thoughts of innovating. I brought up flash freezing, which was new to the world of food at the time. (I had what turns out to be a prescient feeling that finely prepared meals would be the way of the future for people who didn't want to cook themselves.) Naomi could not only help me with the menu for my restaurant, but she had all the signs of being able to create a perfect service operation. I wanted to go into the flash freezing business with her.

We agreed to put something together, but on the level I was considering, it was unchartered waters and very risky. When we finally sat down to put paper to the deal, there was just one sticking point: I wanted to control 51 percent of the company. I had to have control of my risk.

She initially said no. Then without making a commitment, she said she had been seeing a psychologist for years and respected his judgment and would not go into business with anyone until her therapist met that person. I agreed I would meet him, even though we had not yet decided on my having the controlling shares. It's all about seeing the puzzle pieces: meeting Naomi's therapist gave me the idea for my first Drizzler, the medical building. A Drizzler, as you will see, is my pet name for a project that reliably spits out recurring revenue.)

I had never been to a psychologist, therapist, or whatever you may call them. He seemed like a nice guy. He had an old office in a majestic pre-war building on 5th Avenue that I had always admired.

We scheduled a series of sessions to help "clear" me for going into business with Naomi. I was habitually late to my appointments, and after three sessions and one cancellation on my side, it was clear that my tardiness was a problem for everyone, including me.

I didn't want to take any more flak from anyone, and I decided not to go into business with her. I did stick with the therapist, though. I stayed with him for about six years. Go figure. As they say, everything happens for a reason, even his recommendations for me to end my first marriage, but that's another story.

In the first couple of our private sessions, I asked Thomas about his office. Why he was in this space, what made it work, how other offices like this worked, etc. He was a wealth of knowledge.

Thomas explained how important soundproof walls were to therapists. I wasn't there to just pick his brain as a developer, however, and I talked a lot as well (I guess that's the idea.). After learning more about the practical side of the business in the first few meetings, it seemed like a very interesting real estate play. At that time, I couldn't think of anything to do with this notion, so I packed it away and it would come to life much later in my career.

I still had a restaurant to open and had created a friendship with Naomi throughout our dealings. I was even advising her with her business, and she agreed to create a menu for me for the Cooper Square Café. The result was outstanding. She put together an amazing tasting menu. It was also exceptional.

As fate would have it, after all this effort, it all came together. I couldn't have planned the timing of it all better if I tried. We were now ready to open. I was a real restaurateur!

The opening was set for a Saturday, and we were ready to begin the ride. Tony was there with his wife, and my wife, Paula, was there with me. Tony brought his kids even though they were too young to eat anything but baby food.

The opening went very well—with no big mistakes, but it quickly became clear to me what a substantial investment I now had to keep a close eye on. I still wasn't sure of exactly what to look for, and it made me uneasy.

The first week we did great. I acted as host of the front-of-the-room, and I really liked it—it was like being on stage and appealed to the actor in me. I felt like a veritable genius. Money was rolling in, everyone was excited, and the customers gave great praise. I wanted it to be a real blockbuster and go on forever. I was ecstatic and thought it would absolutely continue like that.

We had about an eight-week run of big numbers and happy people. Then the business went into a tailspin. Tony was in the kitchen now, and he came out with the stained apron again . . . and again . . . and again. I couldn't teach the old dog new tricks. My friends began to not accept my invitations—even for a free meal!

People like consistency in the food in a restaurant. With that and good service, they'll continue to come back. Unfortunately,

Tony couldn't make the same dish twice. I guess I didn't ask him if he could do that. The writing was soon on the wall in big letters:

OUR DAYS ARE NUMBERED.

We had such a good start, but now I know that about all restaurants have a honeymoon period for the first few weeks when they open as everyone wants to try the new spot. The trick is to have reviews that get the pipeline of customers flowing. Good public relations sure help. However, if your food isn't good, you're in trouble. Ours clearly wasn't.

Things got the best of me, and I had the nightmarish fantasy idea of making the cafe the worst restaurant in the city. After all, we were on our way. Tony could keep cooking poor food, and I'd have the waiters wear stained aprons and insult the guests. I guess I was trying to amuse myself during this seemingly unfixable problem. It was gallows humor.

The nightmare ended when a broker came in from out-of-the-blue saying he had a buyer for the building. It was like manna from heaven. We all quickly agreed to sell and made a significant profit, happily going our separate ways. I got out of the restaurant business with my skin intact, and my life got back to normal, whatever that might mean.

## Pizza With The Mob

Months later, Tony came to visit me at my office. He said that not working was making him crazy. He couldn't stand it. I certainly was not going back into the restaurant business with him. He then told me that the city was auctioning off leases they held, and they hadn't done that in years. There was this one lease he had sniffed out and said that it was a gold mine.

It was a pizza place right under the overpass one block off King's Highway. I told Tony that I don't like auctions, but for him, I would make a one-time exception. So, on the day of the auction, I sent the shoe store manager as my proxy and promised him a "piece of the pie" (pun intended) if we got the lease. I instructed him that the maximum bid was $2,000 per month. We were either going to get it, or we weren't.

About three hours later, he barged into the office, and excitedly blurted, "We got it, we got it!"

I said, "Great, it's your baby. Now you take care of our partner."

He said, "You know, it's funny. I only bid $1,000, and nobody else bid."

"I guess you lucked out," I answered.

I thought something had to be wrong, but it looked like we got ourselves a pizza place at a great price. A few weeks passed and I was working at my new medical building project when I got a call from my office. It was the shoe manager, and he was frantic. "You have to get over here!" he hollered. I explained that I was in a meeting with two doctors, and he became even more frantic, repeating, "Get over here!"

He had never talked to me that way before, and I told the doctors that I had to leave immediately, and we would need to reschedule. This was a good move on my part, setting the tone of our negotiations. It showed them they weren't as important as they thought they were and that maybe I was more important than they thought I was.

Back in my office, I looked through the glass wall dividing my entrance from the reception of my not-so-private office. It was a lot of glass. Then I saw my manager sitting there facing two gentlemen in black suits that I could instantly see fit them poorly—I could even tell from the back it was so bad. The shoulders and sleeves strained the fabric. (If it was a double-knit leisure suit fabric, it would have stretched and fit them better, I joked to myself.)

Paul, the shoe manager, and now my pizza shop partner, said: "They say that the pizza place is theirs!"

"You mean the one we won at the auction?" I asked.

"Yes," he replied.

I knew what was going on but played dumb. I'm no stranger to improv and I enjoy the challenge of it.

"But we won it, right?"

One of the unidentified men spoke, and it was just like out of a movie.

"You don't understand. It's been in the family for years."

"I know, but I have another Italian family that is depending on this. I'm sure we can make a deal if you need it for your family. I'll have to ask them." I whipped out everything I had ever learned in improv class to deal with this conflict.

"You don't understand that there's no deal," the man firmly said.

"Well, who can I speak to?" I replied. In unison both the guys in the poorly fitting suits moved forward and stared as if, surely thinking, man, this guy must be kidding—or stupid. I repeated what I said for effect and they both leaned toward me together in unison.

Then one spoke, "As I said, this is the family's, and this is our last conversation."

They got up and left without saying goodbye. I said, "Wait! Wait! We are not finished."

Paul said, "Are you crazy? I'm out. I'm not going to worry about starting my car in the morning."

The funny thing was that he always came to work by train. We never heard from them again. We also never took over the lease, and we licked our wounds and kept moving along.

Years later, it was reported in the newspaper that the FBI had cracked down on the country's largest drug ring. The mafia had distributed not just pizza but cocaine in pizza boxes with deliveries all over the country. All of this was coming from a little pizzeria under the tracks on King's Highway in Brooklyn. As I went to bed that night, all I could see were those guys sitting in my office. I got lucky again.

My special feelings for the restaurant business may have come from my grandfather who operated a deli in Brooklyn. As a kid, I remember sitting there loving the whole experience. My taste in food was basic except for those dishes that came from the old country. I loved knishes, borscht, and even meatloaf. Good, solid, old-world food. I guess I just like the business. That's good because I ended up back in it.

## Stand4 Burger Joint (2009)

In 2009, we opened Stand4. And again, I backed into the business. I was a landlord who sublet this space. My first tenant was Kinko's.

It was their first store in Manhattan. Then a very fancy restaurant opened in the location and their very high prices scared all the customers away before they ever even came to eat.

The next tenant was a high-end burger joint. They came in with a celebrity restaurateur. They had deep pockets and were building what they thought would be a chain like today's Shake Shack. It was ahead of its time. Because this location was their prototype, they spent money like there was no tomorrow. Extravagantly.

The tables had brass legs and a special wood top made from rare rainforest wood. They cost $6,000 each. That's just one example of the money they spent putting this place together. The concept did great for eight weeks and then reality set in.

In this case, the real problem here was that the owners were not on-premises. They had created this restaurant with other people's money and expected the concept would work by itself. I have always found you had to have skin in the game, no matter what the concept is. It's usually dead-on arrival if you have no money on the line.

In a short time, they had had enough and threw in the towel. I took back the place back when they owed me a couple of months' rent. I made sure I got the fancy tables in the deal.

So then, I was back in the restaurant business. And I was filled with great ideas I thought would work after my first foray into the business. I decided to keep the basic theme they had started.

The original name was just Stand. I wanted to keep existing customers involved so I called it Stand4. It would be familiar, but different, I thought. Stand4 would be a good branding platform that I could position many ways for promotion, such as "I Stand4 This" or "I Stand4 That." It was flexible.

I got the liquor board to allow us to stay open until 4:00 a.m. I had to give it a try. I was tweaking things. I didn't change too, too much, though I made the bar three times larger.

The existing bathrooms were funny—the women's was very large, and the men's room was tiny. So, I made one, large unisex restroom. I was trying to make the whole place unique and interesting—a Big City destination. In the original men's bathroom, I decided to paint the entire room black, like one big chalkboard. I then installed a little shelf with three pieces of colored chalk so people could get artistic and leave their mark without ruining the place.

Right next to the mirror, I made a sign with oversized letters reading, "REMEMBER THE CHILDREN." I was hoping that would be enough to censor graffiti on the walls. Maybe not. You just can't imagine what people wrote. The walls were covered from top to bottom with art that the patrons had created. Even the ceiling was covered! The bathroom worked, and the graffiti became a dynamic art installation that people talked about.

The bar didn't work, however. I guess no one in a burger joint drinks cocktails. Beer was certainly another matter. We sold lots of beer. I became obsessed with making Stand4 the best restaurant of its type in the business. My creative juices had been set loose, and I began to run manically wild.

I bought a life-size cow statue and put her in the front of the restaurant. She instantly became a popular attraction. Hundreds and hundreds of people took pictures of their children sitting on the cow. One day I wondered what would happen if the cow mysteriously just disappeared? What would people think?

The next day, she did. The day after that she suddenly appeared at Penn Station. The reactions (and the press) were wonderful. Then I arranged for her to make her debuts on Wall Street, in Central Park, and even in front of Saks 5th Avenue. I offered free food to anyone who spotted her and took her picture as proof. I was working social media before it was even a thing!

The cow ended up in the *New York Post*. They wrote that someone had stolen her, and I have no idea where they got that idea. This went on for two weeks. She appeared everywhere. Then disappeared. We kept getting press. I imagined how many kids were crying to their parents because they wanted to sit on the cow. It was great. Finally, she returned home to Stand4, and we had a big celebration that garnered even more ink.

The Village Halloween Parade is an iconic night in NYC. It used to begin in lower Manhattan, and then go all the way up 7th Avenue to 23rd Street, where it turned downtown to University Place. The parade always was, and still is, one of the most scandalous nights out in New York City.

It brings out the wild side of a lot of people, including some normally conservative folks. Men dressed as women, women as men. Scantily clad people roam all over the place. Beautiful bodies, horrid shapes, over-the-top costumes, and of course many, many monsters and a lot of laughter. It was started by a group headed by the director of The Theater for the New City on 10th Street and 1st Avenue. Remember that name—it'll come up again in my story.

Halloween became a perfect holiday for yet another special

performance at Stand4. Word of our celebration spread throughout the boroughs, and people were talking it up. We made a name for ourselves as a real destination. (It reminded me of my young days attracting attention dressing windows in the Roger Garett clothing store.)

I happily got in on the action and had some good laughs on this special night. I always liked to dress up as political figures, just to get the crowd talking. Once, I stuck a mannequin head on each of my shoulders and became a three-headed man. We all had a lot of fun.

I brought in life-size figures of *Pirates of the Caribbean* characters, together with the Blues Brothers, Betty Boop, and many more. We had all these characters sitting at dining tables, except Jack Black, who hung from the ceiling. I had dinosaurs, snakes, and monsters of all kinds all over the place. In the bathroom, I had ghosts, including Casper the Friendly Ghost for the kids.

I really loved Stand4, and Halloween was one of the reasons why. Customers would sit laughing with the mannequins by their sides at their tables. Waiters and waitresses got in on the action, too, dressing up in matching costumes. It was a sight to see for all our guests and customers, new and old—an exceptional and fun celebration that became an annual tradition. It was a great promotion, but it came at great cost for such a short event. It was worth it, though.

We started adding new things to the menu with great success. Different things. I broke every Italian cooking rule by inventing crab cake burgers with mozzarella in the center. All the Stand4 desserts were served warm, even the ice cream. And then there were the milkshakes. The one-of-a-kind Toasted Marshmallow shake won awards, along with our crab burger and the Stand4 burger.

Pat LaFrieda, the premier meat provider in New York, conducted a contest in New Jersey. The who's who in the New York restaurant and nightlife scene made appearances there. Gramercy Tavern, Union Square Café (with Danny Meyer who started Shake Shack), among others, all competed against each other. We were there, too.

Our crab cake burger got the most play in the whole show. It may have been because no one at that time had introduced seafood served like a burger yet. Nobody but Stand4, anyway. We were ahead of our time. We had lines all day long, and they got bigger the later it got. Word was spreading.

In another Pat LaFrieda competition, Stand4 won the prize for the most imaginative burger. No one could believe it, and we drove back to New York on a high. Then reality set in. We received no press, no fanfare, we just got a sign for our window evidencing our triumph.

It was like a famous cartoon in *Mad Magazine* showing five pizza stores on the same block. One store's sign said, "The best pizza in the world," the next said, "The best pizza in the U.S.," followed by "The best in NYC," and the last one, "The best pizza on this block." I guess we were like the second to the last in the cartoon.

One day, a man came into Stand4 by himself and took a seat in front of the open kitchen and ordered a Toasted Marshmallow Shake. Then he ordered another, and one more again. And then he left. My people were in disbelief, no one person could humanly do that. So, they called me to report this strange behavior. I couldn't make anything of it, and I shrugged it off.

I connected the dots when I answered the phone the following day. I didn't know who Michael Symon was at the time, but he wanted to feature our restaurant on his popular television food show.

He wanted "the same as last time, the three shakes."

"Of course," I said. He came with his film crew on a quiet afternoon the following week and shot our segment. It was very interesting.

The next thing I knew we were on the Food Channel on a show called *The Best Thing I Ever Ate*. He raved about our famous shake for about nine minutes, explaining how the taste brought up memories from his childhood when he would sit around a campfire roasting marshmallows. That episode aired for over nine months.

We were getting new visitors from all over the country. Yelp was a blowout five stars for the shake, three and a half stars for the burger. We had a problem that the shake was not very profitable, though. It was so good because the ingredients we used were of the finest quality and quite costly. We weren't making much money on it, but we certainly didn't want to change the shake.

I had to think of ways to make a buck on our headliners. Often, we would participate in shows, fairs, and charity events. On one occasion, we were at Lincoln Center for a cancer fundraiser when a man at a set-up bar next to our booth gave me a vodka drink. I asked if I could buy the whole bottle of liquor from him. That's how the Stiff Shake was invented. I just poured a shot of vodka in a shake and the crowd "drank it up" you might say. You always must explore and experiment. You never know what you'll come up with.

Running a restaurant is truly a full-time job, and at the time, it was not my only job. I just did not, and still don't, trust others to make decisions. I needed to be always be involved, in all ways. It took up every moment of the day, and at that time I had other business to attend to. I truly loved every moment of being there, though. It was like being on stage every night, and I found that magical. It just wasn't sustainable for me.

My lease was ending in about one year. I had other projects taking up my time. I couldn't continue to be involved with everything at the restaurant, but I just didn't trust anyone else to run it. It was a problem. I gave it back to my landlord and rented it to Chipotle. I was finally out of the restaurant business and that made my wife very happy. She was sure that I was working too hard, and she was right. Next!

# The Lift

## Fountain of Youth + Ten

**5**

### 1982

The first Compact Discs (CD) are produced in Germany, followed by the first CD player made by Sony. Spain enters NATO as sixteenth member country and the first since West Germany entered in 1955. The International Whaling Commission decides to cease all commercial whaling by 1986. Ciabatta bread is invented in Verona, Italy, by a local baker. Stephen Spielberg's *E.T., the Extra-Terrestrial*, is released and holds the record for biggest film release for eleven years. Michael Jackson releases his album *Thriller*, which becomes the best-selling album of all time. China becomes the first country in the world to reach one-billion population. Time to lift everybody up!

While I was having my various adventures and business successes in the wild world of New York City real estate development, my parents had continued to work. That was simply the way people of their generation did things. They finally decided to retire, and like a lot of New Yorkers from our neighborhood, they aimed for Florida.

My mom and dad had worked and planned methodically for this move for years. My father was an auditor for the ILGWU. The unions were very powerful back then, and the ILGWU was large and offered its members protection and the security of economic freedom. After my brother and I went off to public school, my mother also went to work at ILGWU in the advertising department. The unions were very good at taking care of their own in those days.

As part of their plan to move to the warm winters of Florida, they purchased a condo in an as-yet unfinished retirement community in Delray Beach called Kings Point. While my parents were one of the first families to purchase there, Kings Point would grow to become one of the largest such retirement communities of its kind, eventually becoming home to over 7,000 families.

My folks spent their entire lives making sure they could take good care of their kids, and this move was the first time they did something just for themselves. In fact, the home in Kings Point was the very first time that they owned property. Their days as renters were over, and I was very happy for them after all their years of hard work.

I guess my ego was getting in the way again, but I was somewhat embarrassed by how little money they made by the time of their retirement. I should have been immensely proud that they raised three kids and did well enough to put them through college. Well, two kids actually—I never quite was cut out for an academic career. It was just as well anyway, and my brother and sister fared well in school. This didn't surprise anyone. Including me.

When my parents were getting ready to purchase at Kings Point, there was a decision to be made: Should they buy on the top floor or the first floor? At the time, I recommended that they go for the top floor, even though it was considered a premium location and cost an additional $5,000 for the privilege. I told them that after all the years of renting that they shouldn't live underneath anyone anymore. They agreed and ended up with a top-floor unit.

They eventually settled into their new Florida lives and were very comfortable. In the beginning, when we kids would visit with our families, there were folding cots and sleeper sofas and complete chaos—particularly for our parents. It started to become like an episode of *Seinfeld*. It was so comical.

So, my brother and I bought several units near our folks' condo so our families could visit without disturbing them. Over the years, my brother and I would buy enough units at Kings Point—at ridiculous prices, of course—so that the whole family could be there together at one time. It was quite nice to be able to connect everyone from up north with my parents.

As time went by and my parents got older, my mother began to have problems getting up and down the stairs.

I said to my brother, "They should have put an elevator in this place. What were they thinking?"

So, with the confidence of a big-city real estate developer, I started an effort to install an elevator. In my mind, it was an easy solution to the problem.

My father kept telling me, "The people here will never go for this."

"So, we'll put in a lift instead," I replied.

He reiterated, "They will never agree to do this. You just don't know these people like I do."

Then he asked, "What is a lift, anyway?"

Well, it's an easier and less expensive solution to install than an elevator.

"They will still never do it," he kept insisting.

My father never liked conflict, and this would cause a fight. My brother Howard and I agreed we should try to pull this together, nonetheless. We were off on another adventure in building, this time in Delray Beach, Florida. This like the rest turned into my job, but we both paid for it.

I called the Kings Point management company and spoke to the head of development. He told me they had once tried to install an elevator without success.

I thought quickly and said, "What about conducting a test pilot program?"

After a long pause, he said exactly what my father said: no one will agree to doing this.

"What about putting in a lift?" I asked.

He said a lift would not meet the Palm Beach County building code. I wanted to investigate this for myself, not being familiar with local rules, so my next call was to the building department of Palm Beach County. They told me you could indeed install a lift if it met hurricane standards.

Now I was getting somewhere. Next, I found a lift manufacturer who said, of course, that all their lifts meet that standard. I then told him—in my best New York City deal-making voice—that eventually, if he listened to me, this would become the most significant order he'd ever see.

All he had to do as his part of the deal was supply one lift in Kings Point at no upfront cost. If this pilot program didn't produce subsequent orders, we would pay for the first one. I made it the quintessential no-brainer, no-risk deal. It couldn't miss!

After I put the equipment deal in place, I went to the Kings Point management and told them that Palm Beach County would indeed accept an approved lift. He hemmed and hawed and said that it would all have to be approved by Kings Point management before anything could happen.

After the fact, I found out why I was getting resistance from management everywhere I turned. They were putting in a separate pilot program for an elevator. From my developer's perspective, I thought management had delusions of grandeur.

They wanted to spend $80,000 per elevator, and there were 800 buildings that would ultimately need to be retrofitted. It didn't take long for me to figure out that this would be a project totaling $32 million, and they would make at least $3.2 million in fees controlling it. It wasn't exactly small potatoes.

Anyway, management wouldn't play a big role in stopping our project using lifts instead of elevators. The economics were hard to ignore by being so much less expensive. Once someone saw the numbers, our argument was easy to win.

That's what I thought until I had to win over the unit owners themselves. This was becoming an entirely new game for me. I started quite a skirmish. The real fight was with unit owners or at least half of them. I never realized this lift issue would turn into a war.

It was all the original developer's fault. They never considered that people would live to advanced ages and that stairs would become a major concern and problem as people aged. It was a different era.

When they originally built Kings Point, they priced the second-floor units higher because the idea that there wouldn't be anyone living above them would appeal to the buyers who mainly came from apartment buildings in New York City. Not having stomping feet above you was a big luxury and a major selling point back then. In the earlier years, the upper-floor owners acted as if they were living in the penthouses.

The idea of a lift as a solution for aging homeowners turned into a war between the north and south. Literally. The people on the first floor were feeling validated by the soundness of their original purchase. Rightfully so, as it turned out. And the people in the "penthouses" were left feeling helpless against the ravages of time.

The entire issue created strong factions between the homeowners, for and against, and it all came down to sharing the costs of taking care of those who made the "poor choice" of living on the second floor. Those on the ground floor had many objections. Some were justified, most were not.

They simply didn't want to pay for it. They said it was bad placement, it would make noise and block their view, and on and on and on it went. Eventually, the situation escalated to a level of anger that would be unhealthy for anyone, particularly for a group of octogenarians.

The hierarchies and factions were forming, and the contention between the sides rivaled anything in modern politics. It was a bare-knuckle fight and a free-for-all between these old people. I couldn't believe it! I thought this was going to be one of my easier projects, but I sure underestimated the resolve of these retirees.

The layers of decision-making started with block associations. The next tier was groups of buildings called sections and then the President's Committee, followed by management. Everybody had a say.

"What did I get myself into?" I often thought.

For weeks on end, it was a hot issue, and the local press followed the fight daily. What is there about Florida? I went to meeting after meeting.

To gain an inside edge, I needed an ally. I had watched Estelle, a block leader, in action, and we joined forces. As it turned out, without Estelle, nothing would have ever happened. She was a dynamo. In her mid-eighties, Estelle was Bronx tough and sharp as a whip. I'm glad she was on my side.

We hit it off right from our first meeting. I was with my father, who was treasurer of the walkway. Estelle was the president. They held the meetings in the walkway, like their own local turf, just like when they were back in New York in their younger days. Estelle loved my father, and they got along famously.

She would always say to me later about my dad, "He was such a nice man."

When something came up at a meeting about a money issue,

she would yell with her distinctive Bronx voice, "NAT? NAT? Where is NAT?"

She was not well-liked outside of this group of buildings, but she sure was a force of nature and didn't care what anyone else thought of her anyway. That's a sure sign of a good leader. She could talk like a truck driver when she needed to, and she knew how to get things done. Boy, did I like Estelle.

When I was back in New York, I knew everything that was going on in Kings Point because of her. We would be on the phone for hours, and she really enjoyed our conversations. Talking with the people in Kings Point was like a telethon, as it seemed to go on forever. I came to learn that when they're alone they don't have much of a chance to converse, so when you get someone to talk with you, they don't want it to end.

I learned a lot about older people during this time and developed great empathy for them. The Kings Point people had worked hard all their lives and now was time to rest. But how did they rest? They talked and walked in a very large pool in the main clubhouse.

There were many outdoor pools across the property, two huge pools at the club plus three indoor pools, a resistance pool, an Olympic lap pool, and a large jacuzzi. Each group of buildings also had its own set of pools. New Yorkers came down in droves. It might have been because of all these pools. That's not so far-fetched. When I was growing up in New York, I had to go to the Bronx even to see a pool. A big treat back then would be to go to Jones Beach.

The clubhouse was one of the biggest in Florida. When my kids were younger, I would tell them that the clubhouse was the length of one exit on the Long Island Expressway. It sounded true at the time, and my kids believed it.

There were shows that happened every weekend, and you would hear the not-so-hushed words, "What did he say?"

It came from every section of the 1,300-seat theater. It was like a comedy routine. I would have hated to perform in front of this group. But it was a way of life for all these old New Yorkers.

I was living in New York at the time, and it cost me a fortune to fly back and forth. On one of those flights, I left early in the morning. I was bringing a surprise for my father, something I did on Photoshop—a computer program he wanted to learn at eighty-six years old.

At the time, Kinko's was a tenant of mine on the first floor of my office building, where the Stand4 eventually opened. I felt if I got in early enough, I could get my work done and drive to the airport. Some good ideas just never work out.

There was a manager there at 7:00 a.m. In the store, there was one customer. He looked like a bodybuilder and that is understating it—he could have been "The Hulk"—and he was clearly angry looking at headshots of himself. I was at the counter and told him uninvitedly that I thought they looked good.

He said, "Who asked you, Jew?"

I yelled, "Screw you" in response. (It was worse than that, but my grandkids will read this someday.)

It wasn't a pretty scene. Now I was running out of time and getting nothing done. I told the manager to get my work out first.

He looked at the other guy, then at me, as if to say, "Are you kidding?"

I had left one of my men in my car, because I didn't want to get a ticket. I got on the phone, called the super of the building, and told him to come to Kinko's—and to bring a pipe.

Sidney the super was a sweet big guy who wouldn't hurt a fly. He came up and stood with me as I waited for my work. The angry bodybuilder went to the back of the store, mumbling to himself and pacing. Occasionally, he made a call on his cell.

My work was finally completed, and I hastily started to leave Kinko's and get back on schedule.

The big guy shouted, "You're not going anywhere. I called the cops."

I ignored him and left with Sidney. As we exited, the squad cars with sirens came from all directions. Cars circled us as if we were cornered coming out of a bank. The police cars were focusing on the two of us. I was astonished.

The guy came out of Kinko's shouting, "Those are the guys!" and pointing at us.

I told Sidney to keep his cool because we'd done nothing wrong. Yet here was a person claiming to be a cop, screaming that he was waiting to ambush me.

I said to the officers, "If this guy is a cop, he should be examined by a shrink before he goes on duty again."

I told them about the racial slur he threw at me and his walking around the store aimlessly, mumbling. I told him that Sidney is the super of the building, and that I am the landlord. Then the cops went over to the other guy. They talked, and he left.

When the policeman came back, he said, "Let's forget the whole thing."

I said, "That guy is dangerous."

The cop replied, "What are you?" Pointing to the pipe in Sidney's hands.

I said, "Okay, okay." And they parted.

Now I was on my way to the airport after this morning's craziness—at least that's what I thought. I looked at my car and saw it up in the air on a tow truck. So, the airport was not next. Now I had to deal with another set of New York City's finest.

I ran over to the tow truck operator and said to the police woman, "Didn't you see what just happened? Didn't you see all the police?"

Then I thought and said, "Wasn't my man sitting in the car?"

"Yes, but he came out when I asked him to move the car," she said. "He said he didn't drive."

I said I didn't know that was a requirement.

As I was pleading my case, my wife, Paula, came down the street on her way to work; she was my tenant as well.

I said to the officer, "That's my wife. Ask her."

Paula was annoyed seeing me still there. Why wasn't I on a plane?

Paula looked at the policewoman and said, "I don't know what he's telling you, but he most likely did it."

Then she walked away; I was dead meat. I was going to miss my plane. Then a New York miracle.

The tow truck driver said, "Hop in, and maybe you can still make your plane."

He took me to the west towing area and walked me in to pay the fine. I got in my car and it was released. While we were driving, he said he understood what happened with my wife—he was married, too.

"I have never seen that happen before," he said. "She threw you right under the bus. I'm doing you a good deed because I don't want that to happen to me."

I thanked him. I ended up making my flight. I called Sidney later to see if anything else happened. He said the bodybuilder came back to Kinko's, staying for five hours and just loitering. They finally called the police, and he left the store eventfully. But he never paid for his headshots.

The meetings for the lifts weren't easy. There was a lot of hostility, and much of it was focused on me. At the first meeting, Estelle got me over that feeling quickly.

By then, the fighting between unit owners had gotten worse—it even hit the statewide newspapers and the nightly news. Friends stopped talking to each other. They stopped going out to the shows. Those who went sat on opposite sides of the theater. It was completely polarizing the entire community, and I never saw that coming. No good deed goes unpunished, as they say.

It took me over a year to meet with the Presidents' Committee, which was the highest court in Kings Point. It had nine members, and each was easily in their mid-eighties and nineties. Halfway through my presentation, at least three or four of the members fell asleep.

It felt like a courtroom; there was someone on the side, writing down everything I said. The committee sat at a long court-like table two steps above the ground with a ramp on one side. I think they modeled it on the Supreme Court—each judge or member had an opinion to give.

During my presentation, I told them that my brother and I were giving the community a lift for free as a test. With those words, they all woke up.

One member said, "Free? Did you say free?"

Free was the magic word.

I overheard one say as he was leaving, "Why free? You don't get anything for free. There must be a catch."

They all voted to go ahead with our pilot project. As it turned out, unbeknown to me at the time, that meant that I had to take a vote of the 7,000-plus families to gain approval. They would hold this vote meeting at the clubhouse theater. We had to advertise it in the local press and follow stringent rules.

The clubhouse theater was a miniature Radio City Music Hall—as I said, it had 1,300 seats. I had to give a presentation from the stage where they had weekend shows. It turned out to be a very hot ticket. I don't know if they charged or not, but they should have.

The owners packed in more than the fire marshal would allow, and it was standing room only. It was the first time the place had been packed since the local production of *Hello, Dolly!* I had never been in front of such a large audience (easily 1,500 seniors).

I regained my nerve when I realized they were all seniors, and besides, most couldn't hear me. It also helped that half were on my side. My presentation went well, but it was the same old same old for me and them. Same pros and cons; at this point, I was tired of it as well. There were hecklers on the other side, which generated the same on my side.

Then it came to me, and I'm not sure where it came from. I said something I'd never said before, and that was the real turning point.

I shamed the owners on the lower level with a very simple and very accurate statement: "You're not approving a lift for your second-floor neighbors. You're giving them a spare tire. How could you not give a neighbor a spare tire?"

The entire 1,300-seat theater went quiet. It ended on that note. The vote took a week, and the lift passed by a large majority. The problem was not over.

We installed the lift to a great ceremony with reports from a local television station and the press. My mom became a celebrity. She made the front page of the local papers and the nightly news. She was the first rider on the lift in her building. It was her fifteen minutes of fame. Then the mischief started.

The lift was breaking down. It was sabotaged by management, I was sure, because they had an opportunity to take over the project and make a hefty profit.   Since I had the inside track to put in the other lifts; they would be left out in the cold. Breaking the lift was like the bad double knits of my past. Here they had all the cards.

We stopped the lifts from breaking down by putting a key system in. We didn't do it for the money.  My brother and I paid $18,000 for the pilot lift, and we offered to do the others for less, but that was not to be. The management company couldn't help but put their finger in the pie and put in all the other lifts for $24,000 each (that was a crime). We just weren't up to starting another war.

In the end, these seniors now living on the top floor didn't have to leave and go into nursing homes because the lifts gave them back the freedom that age had taken away. I know that's what it did for my parents.

While doing research for this book, I found out the lift story went on long after us in Florida. There were court fights between the north and south unit owners for elevators or lifts throughout the state. It went up to a high court, and they ruled that handicap access won the day. It was an unusual battle in my career that hit very close to home and didn't earn me a cent. I was most proud of this because all 800 buildings eventually installed lifts. I consider it one of my finer victories.

## Medical Building　6
### I Found My Drizzler

### 1984

The target year of Orwell's literary tour de force *1984*. Apple computer releases its shape-shifting 1984 commercial for Macintosh computers to cleverly coincide. Prince releases his landmark *Purple Rain* album. Ronald Regan is elected president after trouncing candidate Walter Mondale and Geraldine Ferraro, Mondale's historic choice as his vice-presidential running mate. Alex Trebek begins his long, iconic run as host of *Jeopardy!* Ed Koch is the mayor of New York. The city is dirty, dangerous, and dilapidated. Bernard Goetz, aka the "Subway Vigilante," shoots four young, would-be-robbers. Racial tension ignites throughout the city . . . and spreads widely throughout the country. Time to create a "Drizzler."

I knew what I wanted to do next in the New York City universe of real estate development. Creating a unique medical building became my focus after thinking about my successful experiences developing the co-op loft building earlier in my career. I had learned a lot.

In that situation, you sell all the upper floors and rent the ground floor. It becomes a source of recurring revenue—a real profit center—for forty to sixty years, depending upon the designation of the attorney general.

I call it a "Drizzler" because it keeps spitting out cash flow. In the case of the loft project, much of the street-level retail space in the city was going vacant in New York. These were uncertain times in New York, particularly in the real estate market. My brother suggested we try and get a dentist to open a large office, as opposed to traditional retail space, and that's just what we did. We found a willing tenant and built a ten-chair office practice that included a dental lab.

It was a highly successful solution to the laggard market for retail space. The experience of building specifically for medical usage with specialized plumbing, electrical capacities, X-ray, and soundproof rooms, etc., provided me with the knowledge and confidence to create a unique medical building.

My concept started to take shape, and I began drawing up plans to make a 35,000-60,000 square foot medical build facility. It just felt like the right direction to go, and it guided my efforts. Soon enough, I found a vacant 35,000-square-foot space with options for an additional 25,000 square feet.

It was the perfect property to develop the medical facility I was conjuring in my mind. The landlord was a developer himself but had no idea how to use the space. Therefore, I was able to get a favorable forty-five-year lease, and I was off and running.

I was sitting alone at a desk in a cavernous 6,500 square feet of raw space in the building I had just rented working on my plans. I always like to become intimate with the space I'm working on. It helps me to visualize more clearly in the ways that I process my ideas, and it's an interesting process for me.

There were huge loft windows in every direction. One wall was over a hundred feet long and had windows facing a brick wall about twenty feet away. It started taking shape. I designed the floor with one long hallway going from one elevator and stairway to another at the other end. I created five suites per floor. Eventually, this would become thirty-five suites. I ended up combining two of the units as something of a master suite, so that then made a total of thirty-four suites in the building.

I sat and sat at my desk for over a year before getting the first doctor to sign a lease. Like it is said, the first one is always the hardest, but then some momentum had begun. Word-of-mouth in the select world of doctors caught on like fire, and within the next eight months, the building was fully rented. That is, I'll explain later, except for the fourth floor.

Having a property that was exclusively for medical practitioners was new to me. I learned a lot about doctors quickly—both as tenants and as people in general. In my experience with the medical building, I came away thinking that doctors are a strange breed.

For starters, they think they know everything, but I found many of them to be extremely poor businessmen. This contradictory generality startled me. I quickly found a way of disarming them right from the beginning as we were negotiating. Every good salesperson finds his or her way in a new environment. To be successful, you must.

It occurred to me that the decorum of addressing a doctor as, well, Doctor, creates an instant form of deference for their profession and them personally. It's a forced hierarchy of sorts. I always believed that respect was earned and not just loosely given. That certainly was the case in my own experience.

I began a new meeting with a medical doctor—a prospective tenant—by asking for their first name. This surprised most of them, but they usually did respond. I only had one instance when a doctor wouldn't comply; he never became a tenant. That didn't surprise me.

From that point on, I always called them by their first names, and it worked in a sense of leveling the playing field as we were negotiating. We also had psychologists for tenants, and I found them to be an entirely separate breed from the MDs. They were needier as tenants, and it was usually interesting dealing with them.

We had two psychologists that we called "The Odd Couple." These two took one suite and divided it into six offices. They took the two best offices for themselves and rented out the remaining four. They were dabbling in my business!

Their only problem was that they didn't like each other. At all. Another problem was they had a ten-year lease, and every year I had to take a seat with one or the other and listen to their issues and referee. Now I was doing their job!

I always tried to be a good landlord. The leases I offered to the doctors were mutually beneficial. They got a ten-year lease with a five-year option. I could offer that because I was paying very low rent.

Part of the offer was that they had to design and build their own offices at their expense. At the time that I was contracted to construct their offices for them, they didn't have to pay rent until I finished the job. If a doctor built his office out with another contractor, they would have to begin paying rent within sixty days.

Only one doctor used his contractor. As I fully expected, I got an urgent call from him; he was suing his contractor and needed my help to finish his office, and I agreed to take care of it. He became a very happy tenant.

There was one doctor who was not so easy. He had his wife watch our construction daily, and she would make all sorts of changes. She was nice, though, and she brought all my guys homemade cookies. I never thought of that as an incentive, but I watched marveling at how much harder my men worked because of those cookies.

When it was finished, it was time for me as the landlord to turn over the space. Her husband, the doctor, came in to inspect the job and quickly began pointing out how everything was "wrong." He began screaming. His wife started crying.

I told the doctor that we can fix everything, but his rent was going to start on the clock that day. The screaming began again, and he said he was not moving in until everything was finished. I went into my acting mode and started screaming too, even louder than he. It was becoming very theatrical.

But I wasn't finished; I started to get even angrier, and my men were literally holding me back, away from the doctor. They had never seen me act this way and were trying to prevent a bad scene from becoming worse.

That's when I blurted out to the doctor, "You just lost your lease."

That was always my maximum leverage. It was enough to break the tension, and he settled down. It turns out he was going on a family vacation for two weeks, and he didn't want to pay rent until he got back. You don't have to pay rent until you get back, I told him, but your rent is going to start today, and you will pay for all the work you want corrected.

He said, "Forget the work; I'll accept it as is."

"Okay, you'll sign a release and we'll be all set," I replied.

This doctor was a urologist. And what's more, he became my personal urologist. Maybe he has the leverage on me now.

The entire construction project was moving along on schedule. Then I discovered the reason why I got such good lease terms in the first place. An IMD tenant occupied the fourth floor and that meant an artist could live in a commercial building. (IMD is a New York law to protect loft occupants.) I knew that, but the lease protected me.

My landlord never advised me that they were in court with the fourth-floor tenant. My problem now became clear, and this kind of problem pops up unexpectedly in almost every project. Thinking on your feet is a big part of every project. Because we were building out five suites on each floor, we needed to add bathrooms.

In basic plumbing design terms, all bathrooms must be connected to a vent "stack." These usually run vertically through a building. To add the bathrooms required to service our suites, we had to add stacks—four of them. To add stacks, we had to go through the fourth floor.

Over the year that I had been preparing to work on the property, I thought I had developed a good relationship with the fourth-floor tenant. I advised him of the construction timing and even told him about when I would start. I didn't think there would be any problems gaining access to his floor to begin the work for the stacks. We agreed that we would coordinate the installation.

When I said I was ready to start, the tenant said that he was in court with the landlord and that his lawyer wouldn't allow us access to the fourth floor. I made it clear that I wasn't very happy at all. I told my plumber the problem. He told me not to worry and that he would take care of it.

The next thing I knew, the only stack in the building that serviced two bathrooms stopped working. The tenant called to find out what was happening. I said I didn't know, and I didn't. I told him that I'd arrange to fix it by Thursday, which was three days away.

The next thing I knew, he brought in a porta potty.

I called him and asked, "What are you doing?"

He said, "My lawyer sent it."

"Well, you should go live with your lawyer then. Let your lawyer fix the problem."

Three days later, he called to have me fix his plumbing. They figured out soon enough that porta potties aren't exactly good for showering.

I asked my plumber what he did. He brought me to the third floor and showed me his handiwork. I suspected he was responsible;

I just didn't know how he pulled it off. His work was simply brilliant.

He took a quart-sized Diet Coke bottle, cut it in half, and stuck it in the drainpipe with the bottom facing up like a big goblet. When sealed, it would stop everything from going through. If you opened the cap, you could let some of the water out very slowly. It would appear as if there was actual blockage somewhere.

If the tenant thought I was doing something wrong, he would have called his lawyer, and I'm sure I would have had to deal with the building department. Everything looked like it was on the up-and-up. Creativity sure takes on a lot of forms, especially in the real estate development business.

I now arranged to have "the problem" fixed the next day. My brother was familiar with what was going on and had an idea of how to handle it. I would go into the space with eight plumbers—four teams of two each ready to quickly put in one stack for the four we needed. Like a plumbing swat team!

My brother arranged for four off-duty policemen to be there, just in case. The following day everyone showed up. I rang the bell, and all hell broke out. There was all kinds of yelling and commotion. At one point, the fourth-floor tenant's wife laid on the floor screaming she was pregnant. My brother tried to calm the situation, and the plumbers stood around dazed not knowing what to do next. And all this happened before we even went into the loft.

Within minutes as if this was staged—and it turned out that it was—several uniformed police officers arrived. I thought the off-duty police on our side was a good idea for protection, but I was wrong.

Sitting afterward in a squad car, I found out there was an

investigation about police moonlighting off-duty when unautho-
rized to do so. I was told that the police in our building were
in more trouble than I was. I said they weren't in uniform, and
they were my brother's friends. (Quick thinking on my part, but
I wasn't sure any of it was true.)

We were taken downtown to the 63rd precinct. The tenant
had a grin that looked like he felt he won the battle. They ushered
him into an office and took his statement. I was waiting for over
an hour, and no one was talking to me about anything.

When I was in the squad car, the policeman told me that
someone must be connected because these orders "came from
the top." I wondered what was really happening. I went to the
officer at the front desk and asked when they were going to take
my statement.

He replied, "We don't need it."

I asked, "What's going on? You took my tenant's statement,
and you're not taking mine?"

He said the orders came from uptown. "So, you mean you're
going to let them hang our friends—your fellow officers—without my statement?"

His composure changed, and he made a call. In about thirty
minutes, he said to go into that door, pointing in that direction. I
walked in carrying my bag. I was surprised to see a long table with
seven decorated officers sitting on one side of the table. There was
no chair on my side. I can imagine what they use this intimidat-
ing room for on other occasions.

I instinctively put my bag in the center of the table and
reached into it and took out a Walkman tape recorder. I pushed

two buttons to begin recording, and I said I wanted the badge numbers and names of everyone here and pushed it to their side of the table. With that, a man in shirt sleeves came from the back of the room to the table. He must have outranked those officers seated at the table.

He shut the recorder off and said, "Okay, stop the bullshit. What did you want to say?"

I went through the story, which didn't interest them except when I mentioned my brother's friends, who are cops. Cops moonlighting was a hot topic in the *New York Post*, and I wanted to make sure no one could accuse them of doing anything wrong. He gave me a look like he didn't believe me. I left and went back to the building. I never heard anything about this ever again. All I know is no one was ever charged for anything.

I did find out what "connected" and "uptown" meant. The tenants' legal representation was the firm Vosenholtz and Gadio. Vosenholtz was a lawyer with a very bad reputation for untoward tactics, and Gadio was a city councilman at the time who was running for mayor. So much for power.

I called my landlord and asked him what the hell he had gotten me into. He said we would go to court and get a quick decision. So, I went to court with my landlords' attorney, and we were all in front of the judge. We were simply looking to enforce our right to put our pipes through their space.

I was standing to the right of my attorney. The tenant stood to the left of him. The lawyers stood shoulder to shoulder in the middle. Their attorney spoke first and did what all such landlord/tenant lawyers do. He emphatically described the poor tenant being harassed and put in danger by construction activity and living without water—he meant without a toilet (which was true) and on and on.

Then as my attorney began to talk in turn, the tenant's attorney began to denounce and curse him right in his ear as he was addressing the judge. He could only be heard by the four of us standing next to each other. He was trying to distract my attorney with vile language that is unspeakable here, but clearly designed to upset, enrage, and distract. It was the tactic of a low-life and with each word, I was getting hotter and hotter, and I finally boiled over.

I shimmied slowly over to the table next to him and leaned in and with a low voice said, "Wait until you get outside."

Then all hell broke loose, the lawyer yelled, pointing at me, "He threatened me! He threatened me!"

He was jumping around the table, pointing, and screaming like he was in a grade C acting class. The judge watched it all play out. It did not faze her in the least. However, my lawyer was in shock. The judge said, stop it now, we all know your theatrics.

From the bench, she said, "This case is too involved for these proceedings. I want briefs."

I said to my lawyer, "What does that mean regarding time?"

He said most likely it would take six months.

"What!?" I shouted.

We can't do anything, he said, this is a summary proceeding. The only person who can do anything about this is the judge, and she just did it. As I left court, their low-life lawyer gave me a smirk. I bumped him, knocking all his papers to the floor. I bent down to help him pick them up. He didn't let me. He thought I was up to something, and he was right.

I went back to the building and thought that I still had to put in four stacks through the fourth floor or I would lose all the new doctor tenants, which took me a year to get.

I met with my plumber, and I asked defeatedly, "What can we do?"

"We came up with a plan, which tested the limits of the building codes. My Greek master plumber, Stavros, was able to engineer new stacks to accommodate the new toilets by going under floors, diverting to stairwells, and making unobvious connections."

It was a genius solution plan that eliminated the need to go through the fourth floor. To this day, the only noticeable accommodation to Stavros's save-the-day solution is a slight bump on the fifth floor in front of the elevator that makes people feel like they stumbled on their own feet occasionally.

The building rented quickly after being stitched together, and I ended up running the Greenwich Medical Arts Building for thirty-seven years. Most of the initial doctor tenants did not renew their leases. The medical practice had changed, but the building thrived.

I took over those offices and converted them to analysts' offices. Out of one medical office, I was able to then make five soundproof psychotherapy suites. This enhanced cashflow dramatically. Now it was a real Drizzler!

Our medical building became one of the most significant buildings of its kind in the city—all therapists. It was a game-changing innovation not unlike the computerized knitting machines from my leisure suit era. One major problem with the building was the elevators. There were two of them separated oddly by one block. One was on 12th Street, and the other was on University Place. It's a real thing; the building was on a corner.

One was possibly the slowest elevator in New York City. None of the therapists could complain when the patients came in late—it was always the fault of the elevator. Imagine bolting out from the 14th Street Subway on Union Square, rushing to a doctor's appointment, and arriving at the building only to find out that the elevator was not working. Then you had to go around the block to see a line coming out of the other entrance.

My tenants had good, kind hearts, though, and we became something of a tight community. Often, we pulled together highly successful toy and coat drives for the needy in the neighborhood.

## Thanksgiving Buyout

The Medical Building had been my home for thirty-seven rich, fulfilling years. On a Wednesday night, I got a call from the building's landlord, the day before Thanksgiving. He told me they were going to sell the building and had an offer of $75 million.

In my lease, I had the right of first refusal. I didn't know what good that right was with that sale price, which I considered ridiculous. My holiday was ruined, as everyone I was with could clearly see.

That Friday after Thanksgiving, I started to work on solving the problem at hand. I brought in two brokers and a friend to work on it with me. I asked them to scout the real estate world for a buyer. My right to purchase ended in thirty days flat. At that time, I would have to enter a contract and put-up 10 percent of the purchase price, and if I didn't close, that money would be lost.

To my surprise, many people were interested in the property at that price. I met with Elie Tahari, the fashion designer, at his showroom. It brought back memories of the fashion world that had sat dormant but resonant for thirty years. He was very giving, and I felt an instant chemistry with Elie. We arranged for him to come to the building. He arrived with this tall younger man.

It turned out that the other man was the head of WeWork, Adam Neumann. I'm embarrassed to say I didn't know what WeWork was at the time. They said they wanted the building for the Kabbalah Centre, a religious organization. I felt good about that. I figured a user could make the price work where an investor couldn't. That made sense to me.

All I wanted was a fair amount of money as my return and to create a menswear line with the Tahari label. That really excited me, and it felt like a good time to jump on another train. In fairness, I also wanted my tenants to have eighteen months to find a new office. It all sounded good, but nothing went as planned.

I never got a written offer, and two weeks passed. Noam brought another buyer to the table. We had a long meeting with attorneys present. We left the meeting with a letter of intent. I couldn't offer the building to any other buyer in the terms of that letter, except I excluded Elie Taheri from that clause. I knew that they wanted the property, but they hadn't acted quick enough.

My time was running out. That was a continuing trend. Days passed and Elie and Adam finally woke up. We spent an entire day in one meeting trying to finalize the purchase. At the end, I signed the deal with them.

The person I signed the letter of intent with was calling all day. He sensed that I was working with Elie and started to make offers I knew were disingenuous. They just didn't seem like honest people. I knew something was wrong when they said their attorney would deal with the tenants. Eventually they sued to stop the sale. They didn't have a legal position, but as I've said before if you are rich, you don't need one. All they were doing was trying to upset the closing.

Then the most dishonest thing happened. They closed without me. My landlord of thirty years knew I should have been there. He was only concerned with his money. Changing buyers had changed my entire world. I called Elie and he told me he had nothing to do with it. WeWork controlled the deal, and he had no control.

The next thing I got was an eviction notice. I responded with a Yellowstone Injunction—a legal act to protect tenants—which stopped the eviction until the situation came before the court. Now time was on my side. They had put down $7 million in cash and had a building that they could not do anything with for eight years due to my lease. They would have to close in thirty days with $65 million.

We had our day in court. My attorney and long-time partner, Max Katz, did a masterful job and won right from the bench. The rest is history. I got my money and am still waiting to do a menswear line with Tahari. I believe there are neglected groups of consumers that will benefit from my ideas in the apparel world. Stay tuned, there's another train coming into the station.

## Don't Get Wet In The Storm

During the thirty-seven years that I ran the medical building, it was my Drizzler. The Drizzler is a term I made up that refers to a moneymaker that fuels other endeavors.

London Fog is an outerwear brand that's been around since the 1920s. They also made an outer jacket years ago that I considered a Drizzler. It was a short jacket you could wear to play golf, or just wear anywhere at any time. This jacket was a huge seller. I bet the profit from its sales covered all the company's overhead for years, which gave them the ability to make a whole line of coats and other clothing.

Times were not always good in real estate. There were periods that were horrible for property owners. During those downturns, even income-producing buildings were considered a liability. Four eras when I took huge blows were the 1987 stock market crash, the 1990 overbuilt resolution trust, the 2001 World Trade Center attack, and the Great Recession starting in 2007 caused by sub-prime home mortgages.

Each of these had a different cause: some you can see coming, others can blind side you. I weathered them all, some better than others. I thought I would skip these periods and leave them out of the book because they were so traumatic. The truth is this it is essential to complete the picture at this point.

When you're doing business, you study trends and markets for planning purposes.

But what you can't plan on are acts of God. These acts are not just weather-related, as your insurance policy may have you believe. They can be moved by the governments, whims of the stock market, customers, or even incidents on the other side of the world.

## Baby Bookmark

My first catastrophic encounter was the stock market crash in 1987, which stopped me from developing new real estate projects. That's when I started to develop consumer products instead. These were inventions for everyday life and people, with vast potential adoption. Like many ideas, they came about because something was needed. The problem was no one knew the solution existed, or for that matter that there was a problem at all.

My first one was the Baby Bookmark. I was at the beach on a very windy day. I was reading a book with my colored filter (this will become clear in the final chapter). It was very difficult to read with the pages blowing all over the place. I asked my wife if she had two rubber bands.

I took them and put them on each side of the book and read without the wind bothering me. Then I put down the book and sat looking into the sky and thinking. Had I ever seen two interlocking bands before? I asked my wife, and her answer was no. That's how it began.

At the time of my original invention, my daughter Ilana was studying advertising. She designed a point-of-sale display to sit at the register. It stood about eighteen inches high. A cardboard box printed to look like a wood grain box opened in the middle. So, now you had two half boxes which had shelves on the inside (made of heavy paper). On the shelves were matchboxes placed standing upright to look like books in a library. Inside each matchbox was one bookmark.

Each matchbox had printed on the spine of the book a classic novel's name. It was a small library that would sit at the register. I loved it but didn't use it because it was too complicated for me; she never forgave me. In the end, I realized how incredible the display was. Her creativity still amazes me. Did I tell you she never worked with me again? My clan never forgets; I hope someday she will forgive me.

The baby bookmark never got off the ground so you will have to trust me it was the greatest bookmark ever made. If I say so myself.

## Apple Products

Other than the bookmark, the rest of my inventions were designed for Apple products. My love for Apple started with the Macintosh, and I have every Apple product ever made, including two versions of the Newton.

The Apple computer opened so many possibilities for me that I had never been able to do before, including writing this book. It's facilitated everything from writing with spelling and grammar checks to drawing and designing. Things that were commonplace for most people had always been too hard for me, and Apple products have helped me overcome those disadvantages.

I told you of my disdain for the stock market. That didn't stop me from buying Apple stock when it first came on the market in the 1980s. There came a time when everyone, including my financial advisers, told me to sell. I went against them, doubled down, and have kept that stock to this very day. Today, every once in a while, my people tell me to sell. "It's too much of your portfolio." I buy more.

Since I loved Apple and their products had such success, I created products to enhance Apple's. When the iPhone first came out, it was the first to have a full flat touchscreen. People at that time were used to their Blackberry. It wasn't unusual for someone to carry both phones because they weren't ready to abandon their trusty keypad. In 2012, I designed and patented the Invisible Keypad. It was similar to a screen protector but had "bumps" in between where the digital keypad would display to help guide the fingers to the proper keys

My first version of the keypad was awful, as was the second. The third version was excellent. But it was too late—timing is everything. The proverbial ship had sailed because everyone had grown used to and liked the flat screen. Recently I had an idea to resurrect it for the blind. In this case, it would not be a keypad but raised surfaces to make the phone more usable for the visually impaired. That would still be protected under my patent.

The next was iStrap for the iPad, which was a good idea but had no patent protection. It was a big version of the Baby Bookmark. I did a commercial where two people were playing ping-pong with the strap holding the iPad in their hand. The strap did so many things. It hung on the headrest in your car for your kids, and it protected your iPad, and more.

My current endeavor is the Slide Watchband. Originally, I designed it for the sixth-generation iPod Nano in 2011. It was a cuff-like stainless-steel band that slides onto the wrist without any claps. When I wore it, everyone asked me where I got it. I mean everyone. I never pursued it because Apple drastically changed the size after a year or two and wearing it on your wrist was no longer possible. It wasn't until they released the Apple Watch that I patented a redesigned version. The Slide Watchband may be my last hurrah. We plan to launch the product online as a direct-to-consumer item in 2023.

I've worked during good times and bad for the past ten years, trying to market my products without success. I believe the reason that I've never been able to market these products was because I stood in my own way. I was afraid of being knocked off as I was with the leisure suit. I don't think I've come to that conclusion until right now.

## Real Estate

Another thing that my brother and I did to turn a profit was flip buildings (that means to buy a building and sell it before you close). We did this during a down period for real estate, because that is when there are more good buying opportunities. When people are overleveraged by borrowing too much money, they are sometimes forced to sell their real estate, which is very attractive to buyers.

At one of these transactions back in 1984, my brother asked the bank, "Do you have any other properties?"

The banker responded, "No buildings, but we have a foreclosure of a hundred acres in Long Island."

"How much?" (You know who said that.)

When he heard the price, you could see my brother's face light up. The next day he went out and saw the property and gave the bank a deposit. Then he put together a deal with three partners who put up the money to close on the contract. Not a bad deal on the surface.

The partnership was dysfunctional. Howard made such a one-sided deal they were fighting from day one. He said we paid about nothing for it and owned 42 percent of it. One of these partners, Kian, was from Iran. My brother said that his father was a good client and wanted me to teach him NY real estate and construction.

I was developing the medical building and living on Long Island. Together, with the father, we bought a parcel of land about eighteen acres. We would create a subdivision of nine residential lots. I figured the son could work with me. From the time we signed the deal, he didn't get anything done. He couldn't make an appointment with anyone, the excavator, fire department, or plumber.

So, I ran both jobs, this one and the one in Manhattan. The project was a success, but not as much as it could have been. I let it be a learning experience, and I went about my business. I would never work with him again (I should have known).

One day, I'm on the ground floor of the shoe store in my office, and I look out at someone sitting in the reception. He was not well dressed; he looked like he came from the old country.

I called my receptionist, "Who is that??"

She said, "He says he is your partner."

I said, "What? No, he's not my partner."

I asked her to bring him in. Armon was from Iran, and his first question after pleasantries was to explain that he was my partner's partner and therefore mine.

I thought to myself, "So, what's new?"

He went on to say that Kian built the project in Old Brook-field, and Armon paid him a monthly fee. I was boiling but didn't show it. I never show emotions in a business deal. So, if I under-stood it right, Kian, who I was supposed to teach real estate for Howard's client, actually taught me a new trick. He didn't have any of his money in the deal; that's why he didn't do any work.

When he left, I had my secretary get Kian on the phone. I said, we have an emergency. I need you here. When he eventually came, he sat down in front of me.

He said, "What's the emergency?"

I said, "Something has come up that affects the profit of the project." He looked somewhat surprised. "How much do you think a contractor would charge to put in our subdivision?"

He said he didn't know, and I said, I think about $75,000. Eventually, we both agreed on $50,000. Then I talked about Armon; he must have taken the same acting classes as I did. There was not one movement of his body or his face. It was as if we had met on the street, and I said what a lovely day. While he was sit-ting there, I took out the checkbook.

He asked, "What are you doing?"

I told him I was the GC, and we just determined my fee.

"NO, NO, that's not right," he said.

I responded, "You did nothing on this job, you didn't even put your own money in."

"The investor paid you a fee for being a GC, but you weren't even there." Kian became more agitated. "I was the GC, but I wasn't going to take a fee until I met your investor," I said. "That may work in Iran; it doesn't work here."

In our agreement, any checks above $5,000 had to have two signatures. I said, we can make this easy or not. I can make out one check, and we both sign. Or I will make out ten checks, and you don't have to sign—and that's exactly what I did. It's a sore spot for both of us to this day because we still do business together. He was one of the partners my brother brought into a land deal. That deal took over forty years to complete: a solar farm.

## Museum Court (1981)

We found a building in Brooklyn. It seemed like a good deal. It just didn't end that way. My partners were Al and Joyce. First let me tell you about Al. He was always proper, soft spoken, and dressed well. He also had offices on the eighth floor of the medical building. He was a broker who had a partner named Joyce, and she was his angel.

Joyce was very nice; you could never tell that she was a multi-millionaire. Any deal that Al brought her, he would get half of the project without putting in any of his own money. His responsibility was to oversee the project. I never understood the relationship. I guess she just liked the action.

One day, Joyce and I took a trip to Brooklyn to look at a building that was across the street from the Brooklyn Museum and Prospect Park. She drove a ten-year-old Honda that looked like it had never been washed.

I worked up the nerve to ask her why she wasn't driving a

better car. She explained she was a kid during the Depression. Everyone was poor and out of work, but her father was a plumber and always worked. He made enough money to buy the building that she and her friends lived in. She was too embarrassed to tell anyone how well her father was doing when everyone else was going without. She has always lived hiding her wealth.

The building we were looking at was on Eastern Parkway. It was a brick building about eighty years old with fifty units, only four of them occupied. The subway was across Eastern Parkway through a tunnel. Only a few stops to downtown Manhattan. This could be a home run! Not so fast...

The tenants presented a problem. We just didn't realize how much. I think we paid the highest relocation fee ever paid in Brooklyn. They brought in legal aid to negotiate for them; that was a first. Then the fun began.

We divided the responsibilities as follows: Al was sales, I would design and oversee construction, Joyce would arrange financing and oversee cash flow. So, we were all set, I thought. Then, Kian stuck his head in and told Al and Joyce that I couldn't be trusted (I think that's called projecting). In any case, I didn't mind not doing the work, but I didn't like being bad mouthed.

You know what bad karma is? Well, it followed us everywhere and eventually took over. I'm not going to drag this out. They hired a GC who fell flat on his face and got too much money. I had to go in and finish. This was 1987 when the Resolution Trust Corporation fiasco killed the real estate industry and hurt us.

The bank that gave us the construction loan and permanent loan did not live up to our contract. The only reason we turned a profit was because of the RTC. They were going after the banks. The fact that they didn't live up to our agreement helped us with this government program.

It's funny, but we made the loan with the bank's lawyer and negotiated the contract with him. Then he became the bank president, and he was the one who reneged. The RTC made him responsible when they settled at a rate of twenty cents on the dollar with us. That is crazy, but our government is not known for spending our money well. It took us six years to sell the remaining units.

## Postscript to Museum Court

We never made any money on this project, which we can blame on many things other than the government's ineptitude. One thing to this day that still bothers me about this condo is how we ran sales. 148 Eastern Parkway was the first building that I was involved in where discrimination reared its head.

Around the corner from the building were crack houses that occupied the full block, building after building. It was dangerous to walk down the block day or night. On the parkway where we were, there were mostly middle-income folk.

I was born in Brooklyn and left at about eight years old. Things that happened then only made sense later. There was a practice in real estate called blockbusting.

A broker would buy a house in a primarily Jewish neighborhood. He would then sell to an African American family. He would step aside and watch the word spread of the sale until all the

Jews wanted out of the neighborhood; it was like a stock market crash. No one wanted to be first, but everyone was afraid of being the last. There would be a rush and overnight this neighborhood turned into a ghetto of a different color. Most of the remaining Jews in these communities moved to Queens and Long Island.

This came against the backdrop of Trump's reputation of not renting to minority people. Trump was always a bad actor. With all his larger-than-life projects, he was still a low life. Knowing that he did this as well makes me feel that much worse.

Trump first made a name for himself by renovating a hotel on 42nd Street. At the time, it was a big deal that he played to the hilt. Every day he was in the *Post* with another beautiful woman. He was one of the only developers who played the press so well.

In the background he didn't pay his contractors. There was aways something wrong with their work. So, they didn't get their last check. To this day he hasn't changed his method. During the financial crisis he had to give most of his income back to the bank but convinced them to keep his name on buildings. To the outside world it looked that he weathered the financial storm. And he's still doing this today.

Back to Museum Court, we were in a mixed community, but the whites lived on Eastern Parkway, and the African Americans lived around the corner on Lincoln Place. We had to decide; this building was the first project on Eastern Parkway in over fifty years. We had to control the ethnic breakdown of the buyers. Our decision was discrimination, cut and dry.

Yet in its day, it was just business. Finally, the building turned out to be a mix of 30 percent African Americans and 70 percent white. We broke the law, and we knew it. Today we would have been fined and publicly shamed.

I believe the government intensified racial problems and continue to dig an even deeper divide among us. Segregation wasn't right. I'm sorry for having been involved in this project more now than ever.

# The Russian Connection
## Am I Being Conned?

### 1992

Johnny Carson hosts *The Tonight Show* for the last time. *The Silence of the Lambs* wins the Academy Award for Best Picture. The Democratic Party nominates Bill Clinton and Al Gore for the presidential ticket at their convention. Four officers are acquitted in Los Angeles for the beating of Rodney King; violence erupts in Los Angeles and across the country. DNA fingerprinting is invented. Early text-based version of what would become the World Wide Web is released to the public. David Dinkins is mayor of NYC. The subprime mortgage crisis grows. To Russia, with love.

Along with other notable events that occurred in 1992, the real estate business in the United States took a dive off a cliff. At least that's what it felt like to me from my seat in my development business. I attributed it—as I usually do—to our government's dysfunction and poor management of the economy. I still feel that way.

The presidential campaign was underway and wealthy Texas businessman Ross Perot had thrown his oversized cowboy hat into the ring. Perot was a real renegade, but he was a savvy and highly successful business builder and I thought, like a lot of people, that he brought some refreshingly direct viewpoints to the campaign.

So, when I heard that Perot was holding a rally nearby, I was ready to go and listen to his thoughts in person. As a businessman in the throes of a market slump, I was particularly intrigued by his positions and ready to hear more. In retrospect, Ross Perot might be considered a prototype for how Donald Trump could enter the world of politics as a businessman and shake things up dramatically.

The rally was held in Marie's, a popular restaurant in the West Village. When I arrived, I didn't take a seat. I stood next to the side wall, watching, and listening intently to the various speakers. Looking at the people in the center seats, I noticed that they were from all walks of life—affluent people mixed with the poor along with those more in the middle, workers and bosses and people of all ages. It appeared to me as a real cross-section of America.

As the evening went on, a gentleman standing directly next to me asked, "Do you think Perot has a chance?" I admitted I had no idea. He was pleasant enough, and I noticed right away that he was very well dressed and had a full head of perfectly cut white hair. I guess coming from the fashion business that I always initially judged a person by how well they presented themselves. I still do. We exchanged business cards, and I learned his name was Jack Wise. This chance meeting was our only connection. There were no mutual friends or associates, no nothing, really, just a shared interest in hearing more about Ross Perot and his new ideas for the country.

When I got off the elevator heading to my office the next day, I was surprised to find Jack in the reception area. He was unannounced, and we had not planned to meet when we parted ways at the Perot rally. I wasn't surprised, though, and thought it was interesting that he felt comfortable enough to just show up at my office. So, I invited him in for a conversation.

We talked about a lot of things, but mostly about him. Jack said he had come from Zimbabwe after his family business had closed and was in the States looking for new investments. He mentioned leaving his wife in Zimbabwe and that when he got settled, he planned to send for her. He was born in Brooklyn, he told me, as I learned even more about him. Jack had me engaged, and the time passed quickly. I invited him to lunch and off we went, like old friends.

Remember, my business had ground ungracefully to a halt. I did have the medical building, which was fully rented and all we had to do to keep it operating well was respond to the tenant's requests and collect the rent. My staff handled all that, and I only got involved when there were issues. It was a great property: a Drizzler. I was in the rare position of having a lot of free time, and Jack became a good diversion for me. I was growing quite fond of him.

For days on end, we would meet at my office and talk about

everything: politics, business, entertainment—you name it. I found we had many things in common. One night I had dinner with my wife and Jack. Paula was always a reliable barometer of people, and I valued her opinions and perspective. Women clearly liked Jack. He was gallant and charming as he could be. At dinner, he even read a poem to Paula that he said he wrote. The night ended with my wife saying to me that Jack was very smooth and that I should be most careful in my dealings with him.

The next week was more of the same. We were hanging out together, trying to figure out how we could do business together. Maybe even doing something significant. I showed Jack the Rainbow Reader, my literary aid system to help those with dyslexia. (You will read more about it in a later chapter.)

Jack seemed to think that he could help get the exposure it needed. He said he knew the head of the World Bank from Zimbabwe very well and made a few calls to set up a meeting for us the following week. Just like that. I got excited. This meeting could be the help I needed if it was the real deal. Time would tell.

We flew to Washington D.C. the following Wednesday. When we arrived, I was taking in everything I saw. The building itself was not that tall, about fourteen stories, but covered a whole block. It was pretty impressive. Their offices were not small, and they occupied the entire fourteen floors. One floor was isolated for the executive offices. They were lavish, and I kept feeling better about the whole thing.

The receptionist knew we were coming, and she greeted Jack by name. Out of his office bounded Devan, a large and jovial African man, as if he had been waiting for us. He grabbed Jack and picked him off the floor with a hug. When Devan put him down, he greeted me and ushered us graciously into his office. Right away, Devan asked if I wanted a drink as he poured Jack a vodka.

I said, "Um, it's 11:00 a.m."

Devan said in Zimbabwe it's not, so I also had a pour of vodka. Devan and Jack laughed about old times together. They were clearly well acquainted. Then we began a conversation about the Rainbow Reader—our real reason for the meeting.

Jack told Devan most of the story about the Rainbow Reader, but it was not his area of expertise. Still, he added that he would pass it up his organization to the right people. He tried the test it but since he didn't have a reading disability, there was no difference for him.

So, Devan and Jack went on with their old stories about Africa and the government. Devan explained how he came to oversee the World Bank and promised to get the Rainbow Reader to the education department. I was truly impressed by this time. We got on a plane later that afternoon to head back to New York.

A couple of weeks passed, and I hadn't seen Jack or heard more about our meeting. One morning, he showed up unannounced at my office again. This time he came in with two Russian gentlemen, Turesky and Sadoski. From that initial moment, I had the gut feeling that they were with the Russian mob. I wasn't too far off.

I soon learned that Sadoski's father was once the head of the KGB. He died in the Dead Sea and had worked for both the Russians and the Israelis. It turned out that Sadoski was a very powerful man in Moscow. He and Turesky had formed S+T, a company that developed and built buildings in Russia.

Jack said S+T wanted to hire us to raise capital for their new development in Moscow. I didn't say anything, but I acted impressed with the opportunity of working together with such influential Russian partners. They left the meeting to go back to the Plaza Hotel where they were staying.

When I got Jack alone, I asked, "What the hell are you doing?"

He explained the deal he was working on: We would get a $10,000-a-month retainer and that our job was to attract the finances to help build western-style offices and commercial buildings in Russia. Either side could end the relationship with a sixty-day notice. So, I asked Jack to explain our deal.

He said, "Let's set up a company with the fee."

He also said he needed an office, so we could take $2,000 for rent and split the balance. To me, this was more than fair. We furnished an office and set up shop right away. The next surprise was that we were going to Moscow on Sunday. I was beginning to think I had too much free time on my hands.

As I like to say, it is like getting on a passing train and seeing where it takes you. Only this time, we were getting on a plane on Sunday morning at the Pan Am terminal at JFK, heading to Moscow via London.

We walked up to the British Airlines counter and Jack asked the agent, "Did Sir Colin upgrade our tickets to first-class?" (Sir Colin Marshall was then CEO of British Airlines.)

She tried to be friendly, looked up our tickets and said, "No, I'm sorry, I can't find that."

Jack said to please call Margaret, Sir Colin's assistant.

"No, I'm sorry but I can't do that," she firmly stated, clearly now growing tired of this exchange.

Jack said, "Don't worry, I'll call her."

And he did. After some pleasantries, he handed the phone to the attendant.

She said "yes" a couple of times, hung up, and said, "I'm sorry, we don't have any first-class seats left, but we can offer you business class."

This is crazy, I thought to myself. I had never been in business class before that. It was an exceptional and very high-end experience that impressed me, but I felt something was somehow wrong as soon as I got on the plane. Like Jack had pulled a fast one—he seemed to have the skills for that.

When we landed in London there was an announcement for Mr. Wise and Mr. Rosengarten to immediately come to the front of the plane. Now I was going to find out just what Jack was up to, just like I suspected. I knew they had caught us, but I didn't know just what for. My heart was racing.

The steward asked for our luggage tickets then escorted us off the plane. I dreaded every step until they ushered us into a Rolls Royce and drove us directly to the Churchill Hotel. I realized then and there that Jack was the real deal.

We had dinner together two nights in London, one with an exiled Sheik from the Middle East and the other with an American that Jack said was with the CIA. At this stage, I would believe just about anything Jack said.

The next day we were off to Moscow with a different agenda. We were on a German airline, and the flight was very bumpy and rough. I very nearly used the air sickness bags a couple of times. I was thrilled to land safely, only to see that the airport where we arrived looked like a third-world version with very low ceilings, poor lighting, and exposed wiring everywhere.

I'd never been there before, and it seemed like Russia was stuck in the 1950s. A van was waiting for us. The driver was a handsome young man who spoke fluent English. The view from the highway was desolate. There were no lights and a single billboard. It was for Arthur Andersen, the American accounting firm. It was quite strange, but I never asked why.

The driver, as it turned out, was a medical doctor. I asked him why he was driving a shuttle van, and he said that there were too many doctors in Moscow and that driving paid better. Welcome to Russia.

The hotel, which Sadoski and Turesky arranged, was beautiful and of modern design. It was across the river overlooking Red Square and the Kremlin. I had a suite very lavishly furnished, but its doors were what really caught my attention. They were truly unique.

To describe them, they acted like a bank vault. Made of one heavy slab of wood that was flush to the wall, there were no hinges and no opening around the perimeter. Three heavy hinges were hidden and protected within the frame. The doors even opened with a swish like the sound I imagined a bank vault makes. They were soundproof and about four-inches thick. They were the best hotel room doors I have ever seen. My room was warm and inviting, and I had a spectacular full view of the city.

The next morning at breakfast, I heard the plans for the day.

We visited sites that S+T had built. We also went to sites they controlled—all were within walking distance of the Kremlin. The offices were newly constructed, but they looked as though they were built in the 1970s. There was a lot I could teach them, I was sure.

The next day there was a meeting planned with the mayor of Moscow. His office had one long table on one side of the room with a small desk on the other with many chairs. Our side was a group of five, including a translator. Jack and I were seated opposite where the mayor would come to sit. He came in late with another translator and looked like he just rolled out of bed.

And that was the first thing Jack said to the translator to share with the mayor: "You look like you just rolled out of bed, Mr. Mayor."

Sadoski and Turesky looked shocked; the translator did not know if she should repeat what Jack had said.

Jack said firmly to both translators, "Please tell him exactly what I said."

Sadoski and Turesky looked as if they regretted being there at that moment. I was just sitting there waiting to see what was going to happen—and it didn't feel like it was going to be something good. The translator sheepishly told the mayor what Jack had said. There was a very long pause, and tension grew. The mayor then burst into laughter.

The translator repeated what the mayor said: "Well, that's about right."

From that moment on, Jack owned the meeting. We talked for two hours about seemingly everything, including lumber, oil, and other natural resources. The main topic was real estate, though.

S+T had negotiated a deal with the Department of Construction to build U.S.-styled offices in exchange for an additional floor on the roof of their building, which S+T would own upon completion. The mayor agreed to present this to the committee and said he would support it. We left the office with an invitation to return any time we were in Moscow. Sadoski and Turesky were completely thrilled and impressed with us.

That night they took us to SOVIKI, a Russian bathhouse that was prestigious and very well-known there. Inside, they brought us into a large steam room with men holding banyas, which looked like old-fashioned brooms. When you got overheated, they would hit you with them. Standing there in a towel dripping wet with a husky Russian man hitting me with a broom was not exactly my western idea of a good time.

They told me this was a special bathhouse, the best in Russia and to enjoy it. I said okay, but I was ready to go back to the hotel. I clearly wasn't in charge and instead we went to dinner at the hotel. At least we were away from SOVIKI. The menu at the restaurant consisted entirely of meat. They didn't really need a menu—everyone just ate meat and drank vodka. There were four of us, and we finished two bottles. Every few minutes, someone would say "nostrovia," and we would all raise our glasses to drink, as if on command. They sure like to drink in Russia.

Thankfully, I woke up in my room, but I didn't remember the night before or, for that matter, where I was. I splashed cold Russian water on my face to bring me back to reality. We left that morning to go back to the States with an overnight layover in England. I was happy to leave.

I strongly recommend that when you're in London, you must go to the theater. What a wonderful experience it is. When we were there, there was a show at the storied Apollo Theatre called *Our Song* that starred Peter O'Toole in the prime of his acting career.

He gave the best performance I've ever seen of someone playing a drunk, either that or he was totally inebriated. Regardless, he was on the stage for two hours without a break and was playing it all over-the-top. It looked as though even his supporting cast didn't know if he was really drunk or not. He nearly fell off the stage twice but was saved by another actor.

At the end, he received a roaring standing ovation and had difficulty taking a bow. The audience laughed. His performance that night is locked in my memory and still mystifies me.

We flew back to New York the next day. Sadoski and Turesky were happy with our successful meeting with the mayor of Moscow. Now we had to raise the money and getting financing would be no easy task with Russia's bad reputation.

Our pitch was that the Russian government officials were working with us, and we had an "inside line" politically. Western-style offices were already being built in Moscow then, and the market for them was hot.

They were getting rents of $100 per square-foot as opposed to fifty dollars in NYC for an equivalent space. And the real kicker was that they got an advance of $300 a foot upfront. These were rents that were unheard of in the States. It was so good, in fact, that potential investors didn't believe it. It was too good to be true, as they say. I was able to convince three investors and my brother to go to Moscow and see for themselves.

We all trooped back to Russia to help them with design issues and investors. My brother and the other investors all sat in coach on the flight over. We made a short layover in England and stayed at the same hotel as the last trip and then arrived early on a Sunday morning in Russia.

Howard was restless from traveling and wanted to go out and explore a bit. He was unfortunately wearing a shirt that telegraphed "American tourist" very clearly. It wasn't a good choice, really. I don't remember if I said something when I saw his outfit, but I most likely commented.

We all went from the Kempinski Hotel where we were staying over the Moskva River to Red Square. It took us all of ten minutes. Red Square is one of the oldest and largest squares in Moscow. It is located directly in front of the Kremlin complex.

We were surprised to see the fabled Red Square populated with cheap folding tables. It was hosting a flea market. We were startled by this. You could feel how desperate the people were and see it by noticing what items they were selling. All the tables were covered with household items, not antiques, but electric outlets, faucets, hardware, etc., used and old.

The flea market shocked me and made me feel sad even. That didn't stop my brother from browsing the tables, however. As was his nature, he liked the hunt to find a bargain, even in Moscow! He was attracted to all the junk. Finally, after some hunting, he found a bracelet he thought his wife would like. It was at one of the only real craft tables at the flea market. I watched him stand in line to pay the vendor when someone came running full steam from out of nowhere, knocked him over, and took his wallet.

Howard got up from the ground before I could do anything. I never saw him run so fast as he did chasing after the thief. Thankfully, he didn't catch him since that would have ended poorly.

I went to a soldier who I thought was a policeman. He didn't speak any English. I pantomimed what had just happened as best I could. Surely, he thought I was crazy. Another uniformed man came over, and he spoke a little English. He said simply that there's nothing that can be done now.

When my brother got back from his failed chase, I said, "What did you think would have happened if you caught him? He might have killed you; your money isn't that important."

Sweating profusely and visibly upset, my brother said, "It's not the money—he got my passport."

I thought to myself, *Why did I bring him?*

The investors were shocked yet sympathetic, except for one named Jerry. Jerry just couldn't keep his thoughts to himself, and they weren't particularly kind.

"Are you stupid?" he said to Howard. "You look like an easy target with that shirt on. Do you see anyone else looking like you? Now we are going to lose a whole day at the embassy."

The next day we indeed had to change all our plans to get my brother a new passport. That's not the end of it, though. The next night, Jerry decided to take a walk in the park near the hotel late at night. Who knows why he thought this was a good decision?

A man came up to him acting like he was mute. He went right up in Jerry's face with frantic hand motions. Jerry tried to give him some money because he thought he was a beggar and would then go away. While Jerry was reaching into his pocket, another man positioned himself on all fours behind him. Then, the man acting mute pushed Jerry over his accomplice, and he fell to the ground. They robbed him of his wallet and passport.

When he found his way back to the hotel, reception called me, and I went down to the lobby. Jerry was clearly a mess physically and mentally.

I told him; "You're lucky they didn't kill you. What were you thinking?"

As bad as it was, my brother—feeling somewhat better now about what happened to him at the flea market—and I had to laugh. We let Jerry go to the American embassy by himself the next day. They gave him a tough time. They thought he was doing something clandestine, or they just didn't believe him. It serves him right, I thought to myself.

It was Thursday when we toured the S+T work projects. They were all in some form of completion and I didn't find anything exceptional about any of them—except the rents they were commanding. That still impressed me.

Sadoski and Turesky arranged a meeting the next day with one of the most powerful men in Russia. The mayor of Moscow couldn't hold a candle to him politically. He oversaw all construction in Russia and had been for decades under communist rule. I don't remember his name, but I could pick him out of a crowd anywhere. He stood about five feet tall and weighed all of a hundred pounds. This small man controlled a workforce of over a million men.

This meeting was not like the one with levity that we had with the mayor of Moscow. This guy was nothing but business. S+T had signed a contract with the construction department to build new western offices for them in exchange for the right to create a floor of the same size on the building's roof. Even though the mayor was in favor of the contract, they still needed to work out the terms, which was the purpose of the meeting. Sadoski and Turesky explained that the U.S. investors were going to fund other S+T's projects as some inducement.

Jack and I did most of the negotiating for S+T. At times there were excited, raised voices and Jack and I played against each other in good cop, bad cop fashion. Because of the mayor's influence, we got very good terms on the deal. No one took notes—everything was tape recorded. This was the Russian way.

We agreed on most of their terms, but not all. The sticking point was the cost of world communications because that was highly controlled in Russia. It seems that Sam Zell, one of the largest holders of real estate in the U.S., had purchased all the military's overseas telecommunication rights, and he had not set the prices yet. It was a monopoly from our standpoint, and we were blind to what the cost would be. So, we said the construction department would have to pay for it, and they agreed. That's how the meeting ended.

We had done a good job negotiating, and Sadoski and Turesky were very happy. The best thing that came out of the meeting was hearing the name Sam Zell. If Sam Zell was investing in Russia, it was a great sign that things would work out well.

The mayor of Moscow called us to arrange a meeting with Vladimir Seminoff, the head of the Russian Olympic committee.

Sadoski and Turesky told us that he was one of the most influential and connected men in Russia. Vladimir had never been overtly political and had worked as the head of the Olympics for years, both during communism and since its fall.

At our first meeting, we saw a huge man with white hair and a deep suntan. He spoke fluent English and had an infectious laugh that reverberated throughout the room. He gave each of us a big hug. Other than his accent, he seemed more American than Russian to me.

Then I watched Jack and Vladimir begin to talk about the history of our countries. I broke in to try to bring the meeting back to business. Jack gave me a scowl, which I had never seen before. I clearly ruined his first act, I then realized. Establishing flow is everything at the beginning of a relationship, and I knew I made a mistake. However, I could see Sadoski and Turesky were happy that we were moving on.

Now we began to talk about lumber and oil and other resources—Vladimir was connected to everything, it seemed. After the meeting, he took us out on the town. He said he was going to take us to Moscow's most exceptional restaurant. But first, we went to Night Hawks. It was a nightclub owned by an American, but I had never seen anything like it before in my life in New York or anywhere else.

The bar was over-designed and too well-lit by nightclub standards. It was packed. Not just crowded but packed like NYC during the rush hour commute. There were many beautiful women—mostly native Russians but Asian women too. What seemed odd at first to me was that nearly every exceptionally attractive woman had a sidekick who was quite plain by comparison.

It was an odd spectacle—all these tall, celestial beauties orbited it seemed by these plain, much shorter women. It was like a fashion show with everyone trying to outdo everyone else. The tight clothes and stiletto heels, glittering skin and jewelry, perfectly coiffed hair—everyone was well put-together. Then I put the pieces together for myself. I realized that these were escorts out with their madams or translators. It was show time!

Vladimir pulled us out of there just as things were getting interesting. Turns out that the fancy restaurant Vladimir wanted to take us to was just upstairs. It was indeed a great restaurant, but I would have preferred to stay at the first-floor bar. I wasn't interested in any of the services being offered, but the crowd-watching was exceptional.

On our way back to the hotel, I realized Jack was still angry from my interjection at the meeting. I really couldn't believe he hadn't gotten over it.

He said, "Don't you ever do that again."

I knew exactly what I had done. I broke a cardinal rule of business: never say something unless you have something to add. I apologized again, but I saw quickly it wasn't enough.

The following day, I could see that Jack just wasn't himself. Was this still about the meeting incident? I hoped that it had been put to bed. I needed to know, and I asked Jack what was wrong.

Jack responded, "It's my wife. She's coming to New York."

"I thought you would be happy," I said, and he told me, "I'm not ready."

Jack had hardly spoken about his wife at all up to that point.

Now I saw a man who was so cool in difficult circumstances fall apart right in front of me.

Jack said, "I just can't let her see me like this. I have to have a good apartment and some cash."

I said, "Listen, you can have the fee from S+T. You can have it all until we make a deal as long as the company pays the rent."

That settled him down and we all went back to New York. On Monday morning, we needed to contact Zell. He was one of the richest men in the world. If we got him on board, game over, we had done our job. He was early to the game of doing business with the Russians because he had the smarts and guts to do so.

Sam had a lot of Drizzlers such as publishing newspapers like the *Chicago Tribune* across America, but his main business was real estate. Jack got in touch with his office by telling his story to Zell's principal assistant. He played his first act, and he did it very well. We made plans to meet Zell in Moscow at the end of the month. When Jack was on his game, he was damn good.

Then, out of left field, we got a call from the head of the Russian Olympic Committee's public relations firm. It was a French outfit. Strangely, they requested that Jack and I fly to Uzbekistan in the owner's private jet. Ostensibly, it was to take part in a world conference. We had to get to France to meet him at his aircraft. I was getting used to flying in style!

In France, we met a tall man in his seventies, perhaps. He was thin as a reed, dressed in jeans, sneakers, and a T-shirt, all of the finest quality. He could go anywhere just as he was. Once settled on the plane, he introduced us to four other men. Two were from Egypt and two from South Africa. There was still no exact explanation why we were all going to Uzbekistan.

Then I looked around and saw there was no pilot. The crew was one young French woman offering drinks. We sat for a while in the luxury of the plane, and I asked if we were waiting for the rest of the crew.

The thin, austerely dressed owner of the PR firm said in his charming French accent, "There is no more crew. I'm the pilot, and it's my jet. Why would I let anyone else touch it?"

I asked, "So what about a copilot?"

He pointed to the young woman who had been passing out drinks and said, "She's been with me for years."

That was not exactly what I wanted to hear and didn't fill me with confidence, I must say. Feeling uncomfortable yet wanting to look like a team player, I sucked it up and prepared for the unknown as I had done many times in my career. I was on the train! Well, the plane, this time, anyway.

We were moving before I even had a chance to change my mind. It was a small yet quite comfortable plane, and it was a very smooth trip. We flew about 3,000 miles. I slept half the time, and we landed at 9:00 p.m. local time.

The other gentlemen aboard the plane didn't know why they were there either. Each had expertise in their own country, though. They had real credentials, unlike Jack and me. By now, I was starving, and I was beginning to understand why the owner was so thin.

Two very old Cadillac limos were waiting to take us to our destination. There were soldiers on motorcycles that escorted us to the capitol building. It was not what I expected. All the walls were solid stone, no pictures or color, no details, and eighteen-foot ceilings. We were brought to various rooms that had the same tall ceiling but were maybe ten-feet by twelve-feet in size. It was like being at the bottom of a well. I have never built a building like that one, that's for sure.

Finally, food! We were led to a kitchen and served thick, tasteless soup and a loaf of hard bread, accompanied by a bottle of terrible red wine. The room had one long table with benches on both sides. There was no greeting to us or any form of salutation or toast. When we finished eating, we were sent to our rooms.

The first thing I did there was turn on the television; it was like a TV set that came from my childhood. It was a big clunky wood box with the old tube type of screen. I hadn't seen one of these things in decades! Everything I had seen so far was as much of an anachronism as the set. The TV finally warmed up, and, of course, there was only one station. It aired a Mexican soap opera with Russian subtitles. I thought to myself that I couldn't possibly make this story up, and I went to bed.

When morning came, we were given the same thick, bland soup and hard bread for breakfast. No wine this time, mercifully. We were not allowed to walk outside of the property of the capital, and there were soldiers everywhere you turned.

After lunch—just like the other meals, that soup and bread again—we were ready for our still-unknown task. The six of us were brought into an auditorium with maybe 1,500 people. We sat at one long table, and each of us had a headset for translation. It began with Russian speakers, but our headsets didn't work.

We waited about half-an-hour and then Islam Karimov, the Uzbekistan president, entered the auditorium. He was a thin, short man and wore a military uniform with a braided hat. It was the first time anyone in our group had seen him. He went right to the podium. One of the soldiers motioned that we should put on the headsets. They were working now.

Finally, we found out why we were there. The president spoke to his people and looked right into a camera. He explained how he brought guests from the U.S., Middle East, and Africa to help the Uzbekistan people have stronger ties with the west and other world neighbors. We realized that the only task we had to do was not laugh. It was all over in under an hour. They arranged for a couple of meetings with the minister of finance. Jack sagely advised them to go back to the gold standard. That was that, and we got on the jet to head back.

In flight, I overheard a conversation between the pilot and the ground crew about a man who had been shot on an S+T construction site. Nothing else was said. Jack was still pensive about his wife. He had become a totally different person, and I had doubts he would ever get back to normal, whatever that was.

We still had to make the trip to Moscow to meet with Sam Zell. I was really getting tired of all these trips, with Jack in a fog and people killed on Russian construction sites (there was more than one incident).

Moscow was called the Wild West back then for good reason. Everything was up for grabs, and people were grabbing everything that they could—even if they didn't actually own it. After years of communism, they thought this was how capitalism worked. It was truly every-man-for-himself, and Moscow became a very dangerous place.

Now we were back in Moscow in the Kempinski Hotel lobby to get together with Sam Zell for an 8:00 a.m. meeting. Jack had arranged the meeting with Zell's assistant back in New York and this was the only time available. Imagine: halfway around the world for an 8:00 a.m. meeting.

Zell came downstairs with an entourage and walked in our direction. Jack, Sadoski, Turesky, and I stood there in a row. Had we not blocked him and his group, I think he would have walked right past us. Now it was my time to take charge. Jack was not on his game at all, and I knew it.

I said, "Can we go to our suite to discuss S+T Real Estate? They hold powerful influence from the past regime." I paused for his reaction then said, ". . . which is clearly more important than the current government. They control many properties in Moscow, and it's a very unique position that they hold."

Zell cut me off abruptly and said, "And that's why I'm in communications."

With that, he turned around and left saying he'd see us back in the States. The meeting was over in less than ten minutes. Sadoski and Turesky were shocked, as were Jack and me.

Jack and I didn't talk much on the return trip. When we got in the office the following morning, I could see that he had become a completely different man. By mid-afternoon, he outright killed our chances to move forward with Zell. He yelled at Zell's assistant on his first call back. By mid-afternoon, he abruptly announced he was going back to Zimbabwe. I was not surprised and didn't try at all to stop him.

The truth is I was relieved to be done with the Wild West

show in Moscow and having to deal with the largest real estate holders in the U.S.—who weren't even interested now in listening to our story. I realized then that I was not meant to be a world traveler. Jack had a great first act, and an interesting second act, but he had no third act. I made no money throughout any of this, didn't create a better relationship with the U.S. and Russia, but oh, what a ride it was!

# New Theatre Building  (8)
## Show Business in my Soul

## 2000

America Online (AOL) announces an agreement to purchase Time Warner for $162 billion, the largest-ever corporate merger. The first resident crew enters the International Space Station. The United States Supreme Court puts a halt on further ballot counting in Florida declaring George W. Bush the president-elect over Al Gore. Rudy Giuliani is mayor of NYC. Protesters rally in objection to consistent police brutality and discriminatory tactics. Let's go to the show!

I was spending quite a bit of time in the medical building I had rented. It was convenient to be at the property working out of an office I had made for myself there. That made it easier for me to stay involved in the daily operations, and I've always liked being

close to my projects. At the time, I was also interviewing potential tenants and trying to fill every unit with a number of high-end
doctors.

During this time, I met Stan. New people have always come
in and out of my life around my projects. I like how that works for
me. Usually. Stan was the ex-husband of one of the doctors who
was considering opening an office in the building. He came with
her when she arrived to sign the lease.

He was a big, burly guy, heavyset and with dark thinning hair.
His demeanor was aggressive and argumentative right out of the
gate. Stan was negotiating all the points the doctor had already
agreed to. That's not unusual in my world, so I immediately went
into befriend-and-disarm mode. I was usually successful at that.
It was an especially helpful skill as I attract problematic people.
It was a survival skill.

Stan wasn't just blowing smoke. He brought some compelling questions to the table, and I couldn't help but be intrigued.

"Why should the doctor pay so much per-square-foot?"

It was a direct challenge. No one had ever asked this before.
Doctors who had come looking for space would ask the price, of
course, but they never broke it down to square footage.

So, I looked at him and said, "I don't know."

The only important thing is what the doctor wants and needs,
and the price is the price. Only real estate people consider the
by-square-foot cost. Stan's questions kept coming and I would
answer them simply. I enjoyed returning the ball right back to his
court and was curious to see his reactions to my swift and suc-
cinct replies.

His ex-wife finally said in an annoyed, loud voice, "I only brought you here to make sure the paperwork is right, not to negotiate a new lease."

Stan's face flushed and he didn't make any comments for the rest of the meeting. She happily signed the lease and has been there for over twenty years. It's been a good fit for us both.

Stan was a man with very little patience, I made a note to myself. He was very interested in how I came up with the idea for a medical building and pressed me on it. He was indeed a real estate person, as I had sensed. He saw me as someone who could help him develop a new business model for himself. I agreed to go out for drinks with him, and it turned into dinner. I got the impression from our conversations that he was a loner like myself.

During our dinner, he mentioned something that caught my attention. He owned a building that the city was planning to demolish. Now we were speaking the same language. The building was on the northwest corner of 10th Street and 1st Avenue, he said, and he asked if I would please look at it and tell him what I would do if I owned the property. I agreed to do so. Some of my best projects have arisen from out-of-the-blue. Who can tell where paths open for any of us?

Stan's property was an eyesore and a wreck. No wonder the city wanted to demolish it. It reminded me of those wretched buildings on Avenue C at that time in the city. Inside, one staircase led to about ten small rooms on the second floor. It was easy to see that it functioned as a drug den for squatters. It was a smelly, sad mess.

There were filthy worn-out mattresses on the floors covered

with drug paraphernalia and mold. Portions of the ceilings were exposed, and it was evident by the markings on the walls that there had been more than one fire in there at some point. It was a horrid wreck of a building, but then again, I had never been deterred by a mess like this. I was sure I could transform it into a profitable property. That move is certainly in my playbook.

After thinking a bit, I told Stan that it was my policy to work for myself only and that I did not do projects for others. If he wanted my help, he would have to hand over total control of the development, including the budget, to me.

It was difficult for him to accept these terms. It's hard for anyone to relinquish control, especially in real estate projects. The city had put him up against the wall, and he knew it. There was no other way out for him, and finally, after two weeks, he agreed to my terms.

I rounded up my crew and in a short time, we began the demolition. They did not particularly enjoy this type of messy work, but they were real pros, and I could always trust them to do a great job. Their safety always concerned me—especially with dirty needles, rusty metal, and broken glass everywhere you turned.

They knew their job, however, and weren't afraid of anything. They reminded me of the Native American ironworkers who build skyscrapers and bridges without fear of the intense danger in their work. They too know how to get the job done.

I always supervised the task, making appearances on a regular, even daily basis. One afternoon, while I was standing on the roof, I looked over at a building across the street. Something caught my eye. I was startled.

What I saw was an unusually large one-story building that ran about seventy-five feet on 1st Avenue and about 250 feet on 10th Street. It wrapped around a separate six-story building on the corner. From the street, you would never have seen the scope of this building, but from Stan's roof, it was clear what an unusual giant it was. I came to learn later that it was over 18,000 square feet altogether. It was quite a building, and it intrigued me.

I found out that during the Great Depression, it was used as a city-run food market. Now, the building was divided into six non-profit theaters, operating as an incubator for new playwrights. As I set out to learn more about this interesting property, I learned that the leaders of the group that ran the theater were a bit eccentric with an added bit of erratic thrown in, to put it nicely. All this was right in my wheelhouse, and I got very excited and wanted to learn more still.

Upon making an appointment with the theater group, I walked straight through the open, roll-up garage door entrance. It was like a large warehouse, painted all gray and with very little natural light. The ceiling soared to eighteen feet and higher in places. I was standing in a large hallway when I was greeted by the director in charge of the theater group. Her name was Cristal. She was a middle-aged woman with a powerful gaze and piercing eyes that seemed to look right through you. I explained that I was renovating the building directly across the street. Cristal engagingly took me on a tour of the building.

The first stop was a stage that had nearly thirty-foot-high ceilings. It seated 300 people and had recently been constructed. I was impressed. Then Cristal showed me five smaller theaters that held anywhere from fifty to one hundred patrons.

The group was positioned to stage a play of almost any size and that pleased the actor in me. After my career in textiles ended and I was exploring other options, I took up acting classing. I was mentored by the legendary Lee Strasberg, who taught James Dean, Marlon Brando, Paul Newman, and many more wildly successful actors. While it was a joy to perform, I felt it was too risky to pursue it as a career. I took what I learned and applied it to other situations, as you know by now.

While on the tour I met the second-in-command, an artistic-looking fellow named Marc. They both seemed lovely. My experience told me that that's a cue for me to be very careful around them and that first impressions can be very misleading.

I told Cristal and Marc about myself and some of my development projects. Along the way, I made sure to emphasize my background in acting on the stage in plays like *The Typists and The Tiger, Hello Out There!* and *Death of a Salesman* and my love of the arts. I could see that offering myself in this way was a real icebreaker. It was also true.

I love the theater, and I'm sure that was clear to Cristal and Marc. I have always found acting to be an absolute and complete joy. Being on a stage was my first love. I found it magical to be able to create in such a manner. I thought we all hit it off well, but I certainly didn't know where it all might lead—if anywhere.

I kept thinking that Cristal looked like an extra in every movie I had ever seen. She had landed some roles in a few Woody Allen films, but mainly she was an actress who had devoted her life to these six stages we were standing by. Cristal handpicked every play, and with six stages available, there was a lot of work required to keep everything running smoothly. The place hardly ever had a dark night.

This was no amateur operation. The theater's board of directors was a dream team led by Tim Robbins and Edward Albee, along with many other high-profile artists. Everyone involved in the organization looked like they were just waiting for their shot in the big league—a spot on Broadway. This included Cristal and Marc, too.

Marc took care of everything in the building, and he could answer any question about it. He was built like a tree trunk. Unmovable, he seemed. He had played roles in movies with De Niro and Pacino. That made sense.

It was 1998, and the Theater for the New City (TNC) was going to be foreclosed on by a private contractor. After navigating a major renovation, the money ran out when grants for the arts stopped abruptly. They had plans to build a 10,000-square-foot building and were now prepared to sell those rights.

It was a rare opportunity, and I didn't want to let it slip away. I spoke to a friend who was an architect for some informed input. I felt we could build a much larger building based on the size of its footprint. After digging a little deeper, I found out that the building had air rights. This was pure gold. I could build as high as the code would allow and thought I'd be able to erect an additional 35,000 square feet, at least—but I knew I could get away with a lot more than that.

The TNC needed to move quickly, and we were able to work out a deal that seemed good for everyone. Soon afterward, my brother and I handed Cristal a signed letter of intent along with a check for $30,000.

The following morning, we were going to formalize the deal. My brother brought a friend who was also an attorney to the meeting. His sole duty was to come with us to finalize the deal and make it official. That's all he was supposed to do. As the meeting progressed, we learned that the TNC did not in fact own all the air rights they had claimed—only the first eight feet above the roof.

"I've heard enough," our lawyer surprisingly announced.

I was shocked and mortified when he picked up his bag and oddly stormed out the door. I couldn't believe he did this, and it certainly didn't look good for us. I was the client. If anybody was going to end the talks, it should have been me.

I covered up for his abrupt exit and did damage control to wrap up the deal by offering an additional $30,000. It worked. Now we had control of the property. By law, when you sign a real estate agreement and the money you put down is accepted, you then have total control of what happens to that property from that moment. It's called a Lis Pendens (a Latin term translated as a pending legal action), which prevents any other buyer or seller from marketing or purchasing the property. We used a similar letter of intent for the medical building.

To try and find out where things stood with the property, I met with the city officials who oversaw preserving the arts. They were behind our buyout, mainly because the city had no money (nor did the federal government), but they wanted to make sure the property remained as a home for the arts.

In fact, the one-and-only condition they had was that the TNC stay in operation. I knew that would be the case—the building was an established, iconic arts center, and we would support it remaining so. It was not a designated landmark building but preserving for the arts was imperative. I was all in for that.

About a month after the signing, the Theater for the New City did something very strange and unexpected. They made the foolish mistake of entering into an agreement with another buyer. They also took money from them, which created an even bigger problem.

The Board of Directors from the theater came to my office with the new buyer and said, "You need to step aside from this deal. After all, we all want to save the theater." I responded dryly, "I'm not sure why you did that. What you did was put a nail in a coffin for the theater."

I didn't take any calls for a week. Silence can be a very powerful communication tool. Finally, the other buyer, Phil, reached out on his own and pleaded with me to give up on the deal. I said there was no way I was backing out and warned him that if he continued on this path the city would have to put the building up for public auction. Neither of us would get it if that happened.

We were moving ahead with the plans for the building. Now I had to find a partner who actually builds buildings. That wasn't hard to find, though. In this arena, everyone is looking for a piece of the pie.

I was at a cocktail party at my friend Antonopoulos's home when I met Eric. He was an affable Greek man who was a very well-known builder in the city. He was a large man, and I noticed that he liked to hug a lot. I described the deal to Eric, and he jumped right in and said he would do it. Just like that!

The difference between Eric and other partygoers I've known is that he actually did what he said he'd do. He was all in for real. That was very refreshing. We worked it out that he would build the property, I would market it, and we would split the profits 50/50. It was just that easy to cut the deal with Eric.

Now, all we had to do was close on the property. What I predicted happened. The city put out a Request for Proposal (RFP), which was the same thing as a public auction with written bids. At least now I was ready if we ended up finally acquiring the property.

Then something unthinkable happened. TWA Flight 800 exploded and crashed into the Atlantic Ocean twelve minutes after taking off from JFK Airport. All 230 people aboard the flight were killed, including my new business partner, Eric.

It was all over the news of course, and speculation about the cause of the explosion was far-reaching, including the rumor that it was shot down by someone with a rocket launcher on a beach on Long Island—possibly an act of terrorism. The investigation went on for four years and was the most extensive and costly air disaster investigation in U.S. history at that time.

When the final report was made, it stated that the likely cause was an explosion of flammable fuel vapors. I was in complete shock after the tragedy and wasn't quite sure how to process losing my great new partner.

I reached out to his company, and they were in deep water trying to do their own processing of loss and figuring out how to manage Eric's current obligations. My project couldn't possibly fit into their agenda, and I completely understood that. I offered to help them with whatever I could to keep the deal alive, but it was clear that wasn't going to happen.

I was on my own for this project. I knew that for sure. Sometimes I wonder what great things Eric and I could have accomplished together.

Time to figure out what I wanted to do. I would lose the construction loan I had worked so hard to obtain, and I still didn't have a deal. Without my construction collaborator, I was flying solo without building experience, but hey, that had never stopped me before.

I had big points in my favor. Included in the RFP was the necessary disclosure that the building was under foreclosure and that there was a potential lawsuit that might follow. These two liabilities would be transferred with the property to any new buyer. No one wanted to take on these burdens, and there were few participants in the bidding. The city manager called me on Saturday morning after they received all the bids.

Surprisingly, I was invited to increase my bid. It was a very unusual and gutsy request—if not completely against the law. I guessed that they preferred me to the other bidders. At this point, I had no intention of allowing this to fall out of my hands, so I raised my offer by $500,000. My bid was now up to $1,100,000 from $600,000. Out of left field, I got an aggressive call from Phil, the "other" buyer. He wanted to buy me out.

"No!" I snapped at him. "You've already cost me $500,000."

He softened his tone immediately. "Let's have lunch, I'll buy," he said.

I like doing deals at lunch, so I agreed to meet. It felt like we were on a date. Phil was as charming as could be and made me an offer I couldn't refuse. Why do I always fall for it? He would take on all the construction requirements as well as arrange the necessary financing. I would get 50 percent of the profits once it was completed.

We negotiated a partnership, on the condition that I design the build-out. I was going to make the building twice the size, and he had planned row housing. I wanted to create a structure the likes of which no one had constructed on the East Side for over seventy years. I explained that we would have unobstructed views of the World Trade Center and spectacular views in all other directions.

When Phil and I shook on these plans, my responsibilities included preparing a specialty foundation that would support the increase of the size of the building and Phil would deal with the rest of the structure. The foundation work was very complex, and I had compound ignorance—I didn't know what I didn't know.

My engineer, Joe, was not very excited about my idea for the foundation. That's a massive understatement. Joe informed me that at the building's location on the Lower East Side, there were canals running underground everywhere. He explained that the foundation that I was considering would crumble and not have the strength to hold a tower of the magnitude I had envisioned.

We had to conduct a boring test to determine exactly where we stood empirically. A boring is a metal tube pounded into the ground. You hope to hit bedrock. If you do strike bedrock, everything is okay to carry a building. If there's no bedrock, then the dirt below has to support the building. You also need test borings to learn the strength of the dirt. We did not pass the test.

The ground was too weak to support a high rise, hence the reason there are so few tall buildings in the East Village. So, naturally, I found another engineer. I really wanted to get this done . . . my way. I brought the results of the test to the new engineer, Gregory. He said he could do it, but the cost of construction would be prohibitive.

"Let me be the judge of that," I countered.

Beyond the high cost, the job was no easy task. We had to pour a slab of concrete with a rebar about six feet deep. That was completely unheard of at the time, and only used for buildings three-to-four times the size of our project. We were killing an ant with a bazooka, but it had to be done.

Gregory offered one other solution to the problem that was less expensive, but its methods would have conflicted with my agreement to keep the theater open throughout the year. I was allowed only two months for the theater to go dark during construction. Time was my enemy and I had to make moves quickly. I needed to start digging.

My friend Sal lived on Long Island with his family. Sal was a house framer and a guy I trusted. He had a heart as big as the houses he built. He was a real leader, too, and I knew he could be the guy to supervise the foundation job. Sal would handle all the other workers around him.

In my experience, whether he yelled, threatened, or just simply directed the work, the job would get done, and the final product always resembled perfection. Sal had an aggressive personality. That's how he got things done, and I was glad he was part of my team.

Construction had to proceed without disrupting the theater's shows. This was a real logistical problem that I had to figure out fast, and it kept me up all night for days. One night while I was walking around the site, two words popped into my head and out of my mouth that would have a tremendous impact.

"Conveyor belt!" I announced.

We had to remove 5,000 square feet of soil with a conveyor belt. The men thought I was crazy, but I thought I was brilliant. They could be as loud as they wanted while digging out the basement during the day. At about 7:00 p.m., the shows would go on as usual. Sal and I designed a system where only we knew what was truly happening there. We set up a conveyor belt and carried the dirt to a dump truck, filling a new truck every two hours. This continued for three months without a hitch.

There was only one small interruption throughout the process. One section—about 1,500 square feet on the lower level—had to be excavated to a depth of fourteen feet. We didn't have the time to complete this within the month before the theater was scheduled to be in full operation.

I kept reaching into my creative book of tricks and brought in a tractor with a giant bucket attached. It was the size of a small truck. It built its own road to make runs into the hole to get loaded with dirt, which it would carry back out to a dump truck. Then it would return to the hole. And so on. It worked perfectly for the first couple of weeks, right until the very last few loads. The tractor took out the path it was using and found itself in the hole without a means to get out—not unlike painting yourself into a corner while painting a floor. Sound stupid? It was.

Now we still had to get the tractor out of an eight-foot-deep pit. It was trapped, and there was absolutely no space to situate a crane large enough to lift it out. We were in a hole—literally.

Everyone on the job had an idea that they claimed was the best solution to the problem, but every one of those ideas was also extremely dangerous. It was really a matter of how many men would be at risk. We agreed on one idea that would require precision maneuvers from the tractor driver. It made me anxious just thinking about it.

We ended up renting a small crane to fit in our tight spot, but it just didn't have the muscle needed to lift the entire tractor out. But we tried. The driver of the tractor said he had a new plan and walked over to the crane operator. They talked for a few moments. It was like a catcher going to the pitcher's mound to discuss a plan of attack. I watched from afar as the operator of the tractor shook his head "no" a few times and then smiled and nodded silently. They asked that everyone go to one side of the floor. I had no idea what they were going to do.

It was unlike anything I'd ever seen. The first stage of the plan was for the crane to first detach the bucket and then fasten a cable to the top of the tractor as a safety precaution. If this did not work, both the tractor and crane could come crashing down. I didn't even want to think about what could happen to the operators.

Next, the driver of the tractor needed to speed across the floor of the pit toward the eastern wall. He would then use the cleats on the tractor to vertically climb the wall. The cable from the small crane would help support and steady the tractor as it tried to climb the wall. It would also provide some lift too. The tractor was going to have to do most of the work, though. That was the plan, anyway.

Finally, the driver hit the gas and accelerated toward the wall. I watched and held my breath. When it hit the wall head-on, with the support of the cable on top and the speed of the cleats, the tractor climbed up wall. When it reached the top, the tractor flew like a rocket across the first floor of the theater lobby. The crane's cable reduced the momentum, like a parachute tethered to a drag racing car. I began breathing again. We did it. Everyone cheered. This certainly broke every OSHA rule and could have gotten us shut down for good.

One week later, Phil and I worked with our architects to finish the final design of the building. Thankfully, Phil was not involved with the foundation work, and I certainly didn't bring him up to date on the daily shenanigans we employed to get the job done. We both met with the engineer and architect to finalize the plans. Toward the end of our meeting with these important project professionals, Phil got so frustrated for some reason that he stood up and shouted, "You fuckers are all fired!" and stormed out of the room.

Everyone's jaws were on the floor. I was beyond stunned. I quickly gained my composure and very calmly directed the team crew to disregard him so we could finish the meeting. We continued and settled on a set of plans. I would find out what happened to Phil later.

Phil's tantrum was unprovoked and came out of nowhere. I couldn't imagine anyone acting that way—and I've seen a lot of unusual behavior, including my own. I needed to know what had just happened. Phil finally called to apologize, and he explained that these professionals—jerks, as he called them—were hurting him on another project.

"Phil, you recommended them to me. What happened? We are too far into this project to change the plans now." I told him not to come to any more meetings until he had settled his other affairs, and I would keep him informed.

Soon afterward, I got a call from Phil asking me to meet him at his lawyer's office. I asked him why and he said he needed my help. I had met his lawyer, Howard, when we originally negotiated the deal.

Howard was a small man and very mild-mannered. My sense of him was that he was more devious than he was competent and that I had to be on the lookout for any tricks he might have. So, I got on the subway to get across town to the meeting and kept reminding myself to stay alert and on my toes throughout the meeting. When I got there, Phil was in the waiting room.

I sat down next to him. Phil got up and asked me to follow him. I exchanged greetings with his lawyer and sat down at his conference table. Phil asked Howard for "his file" and this was denied. He asked me to step outside, and I did. This all happened within two minutes of entering the meeting room.

Phil was a big boy and perfectly bald. He was rather scary-looking and had an aggressive and brash persona to match. He had been in the building industry for many years after inheriting the family business when his father died. He was not a guy to play around with. That was clear to me.

As I left the office, I heard the door lock behind me. In a few seconds, I heard screams coming from inside.

It was Howard saying, "I don't have the files here."

"You're lying."

"Don't hit me!"

This sounded serious and I tried to get in the room by battering the door with my shoulder—like in the movies. I took a step back when Howard's partner, a former Marine, came running from the adjoining office and shoved me out of the way. Not only did he bust the door open, but he took down the entire metal frame along with it.

My eyes widened as I tried to understand just what I was seeing when the door opened: Phil was holding Howard up against the wall by his neck, about a foot off the ground. When he saw Howard's partner with a baseball bat in his hands, he let Howard down gently. The police were on their way, Phil was told.

Phil sprinted out of the room and headed straight down to his car, which was parked right in front of the building. He got in the driver's seat and just sat there. The whole scene was surreal. The NYPD came and went down to the car, arrested him, and took him away. It seemed like a good idea for him to spend a night in a cell and cool down, I thought.

When I called the following day to check up on him, I learned that he was still in the slammer. I decided to go downtown and bail him out. I guess I have a thing for strays.

I looked Phil directly in the eyes, and said, "In just two meetings, you have turned our entire project upside down, and I don't get why."

I felt a slight bit of empathy when he explained that his errant behavior was due to his reliance on medication. Without it, he had no control over his temper.

"Why wouldn't you take your meds?" I asked.

"It kills my sex life," he said sheepishly.

What a day I was having!

Okay, now I at least realized what was going on: Phil was crazy and uncontrollable when he didn't take his meds. He was also my partner in this major project. It was unsettling.

I told him, "If you're going to work with me, you must stay on your medication, period."

What else could I say? He apologized and agreed.

We held weekly meetings with the two general contractors working with us on the project. At the third meeting, Phil was losing it again. He began wildly shouting at one of the contractors who then threw his cell phone like a rock at Phil's bald head. Phil ducked and the projectile broke the glass window of the trailer that housed our office. Phil was out of his depth, though. These GCs weren't college-educated, they were street smart, and they certainly didn't take any crap like that from anyone.

Phil left and I told the general contractors to never let him back on the job site. From that point on, security had him banned from the property. You can't make this stuff up, as they say.

To add to my problems, my high-priced architects said they had made a mistake. The code required a thirty-foot setback from the twelfth floor to the top of the building. All the plans had been approved and now had to be reworked. We would now have to refile and would lose time and money because of their mistake.

I was not happy and set out to consult with another architect. Roberto was a smooth-talking and suave Italian who really knew his field expertly. I told him the problem, and I suggested that we could move the square footage to the top of the building and solve the problem. I could have kissed him when he told me that surely it could be done.

Roberto was a one-man show, and he was able to think on his feet and make magic. He said we can add an additional 3,000 feet to the building. He explained that most large architectural firms don't try to get you the most square footage because they don't want to push the envelope. I, on the other hand, don't mind pushing the envelope—especially when I know I'm right. Succinctly, we played with the designations of over 300 mechanical rooms in the building and "found" our extra 3,000 square feet.

Roberto lived up to what he said we could do and solved the problem to everyone's relief. He became my only architect from that day forward. I've always rewarded smart, out-of-the-box work with loyalty.

I really love and enjoy the process of building. You create something out of nothing, like magic, and it all comes together. Where would any great city be without developers who are willing to stretch boundaries and say yes, when everyone else is shouting NO! I guess you would have to have a larger-than-life personality to build a structure like the Chrysler Building.

Back at our site, as mentioned earlier, we had to pour that huge concrete base for the foundation to make up for the lack of bedrock as a footing. Now, it was beginning to come to life as we started to pour the foundation. It was a six-foot-thick maze of rebar crisscrossing and layering every foot for 5,000 feet. Tons and tons of cement had to be delivered, poured, and vibrated throughout the maze of rebar in just one continuous pour.

Hundreds of cement mixing trucks lined the roads from 10th Street to 2nd Avenue to 11th Street and to 1st Avenue to do the full pour. As one truck left its load, it was followed by the next and then the next for over forty-eight hours, each truck doing a pivot turn around and then across the Brooklyn Bridge or Manhattan Bridge to refill and return to the site. Twenty men helped the concrete cure, using racks, rebar, and two by fours. It was the closest I ever got to an Army maneuver. Try imagining all this action taking place in the middle of New York City.

We successfully completed the foundation, and it was now time for the next phase: dropping fifteen steel columns in a two-month period—all without blocking any views of the six theater stages. Building a seventeen-story tower over an audience was the most challenging part of the project. It was preposterous, really. If I had been a more experienced builder, I wouldn't have even tried to do such a thing.

Every major construction project comes complete with unique and unexpected problems that require equally unique solutions and ours was certainly no exception. For starters, the roofs over the stages had to be water-tight, and they weren't. This was a critical problem.

After playing around with assorted fixes for the roof leaks, I dreamed up a system using tarps to make a basin with a drain—like a sink—that used golf and tennis balls as filter media to stop construction debris from clogging it up. It was a real Rube

Goldberg contraption, and it worked like a charm for the life of the project. I don't think they're teaching that play in any architecture school, and there were other equally creative ideas that brought the project to completion.

I brought in a crane to erect fifteen steel columns that would hold a platform. From that platform, we would build the new seventeen stories. We would construct the structure like a giant erector set. The building was not square. It had eleven corners and four more with elevator shafts. A column was needed at each corner.

These columns were anchored to the beautiful new concrete slab in the basement and penetrated the roof. The first floor of the new building would be the third floor of the theater. The new superstructure was appropriately given the nickname "The Lollipop" because I had to keep the "stick" on the first floor, the beams that held up the building floors and the tower were all above the theater.

I found myself by necessity executing everything that my partner Phil promised he would take care of. I had to. One challenge was that all the building materials had to be light in weight, not like standard construction. Exterior walls could not be made of brick or glass.

I found a company that manufactured prefab curtain walls that were half the weight of most other products. They were manufactured at an old Grumman airplane hangar in Long Island, New York, right nearby. This was an experimental material at the time, but revolutionary. I studied some samples of the walls on a building in New Jersey as this new curtain wall product had never been used before in NYC.

We ended up constructing a two-story walled "building" that was used to test the material for water tightness with windows. It looked like a giant box. There was a crowd of engineers gathered at our testing site to certify the results and get approval to use this radical new material in NYC. The various demanding tests were very successful. We went into fabrication and were on our way. Again. You can always make the pieces fit if you try!

Now we were ready to erect the new TNC building. We absolutely needed a crane, and the cranes were all unionized. By now, you know how I feel about unions. It's not a good feeling. Union cranes were the only game in town, too, and we would certainly end up having a union crane at our site. Another problem was that when you used a union crane, all the other tradespeople, such as electricians and plumbers, had to be union shops as well. They keep it in the family.

If you tried not to use union shops, they would picket the site, and no one would cross the picket line. Then the union crane operator would cease working, too. The mob had always controlled the union, but I had a workaround.

Remember, we had two entrances at the property, around the corner from each other. We had all our nonunion tradespeople enter the job through the door on 1st Avenue, so they didn't have to cross an imaginary line. No one could picket us. We had a union crane on 10th Street.

This ploy worked very well for quite some time, until one day it was discovered, and I got a call from another trade union. This wasn't going to be good; I was sure. I had spent most of that day in an unheated construction shed at the job site, watching the action. We were in the thick of a freezing New York winter. I ended up sick with the flu and was forced to take a few days off to recover in bed.

I was all bundled in, nice and warm, watching the five o'clock news. I was processing how I was going to handle the other trade unions finding out how I had skirted them. Then my world changed again. A breaking story about a crane falling in NYC was unfolding, live.

As I watched, I remember feeling sorry for the people running that job. I was relieved to learn that no one was hurt. Then they said something that sent a cold chill up my back: "East 10th Street." Holy shit! That was MY site!

I jumped out of bed and walked the twelve blocks to my site. It was cold and dark. Fire trucks and police swarmed the area with sirens blaring. Reporters were interviewing everyone and anyone. The mast of the crane had toppled over onto the building, knocking out three floors of plank. I freaked out.

"How could this happen?!" I yelled to myself.

My general contractor, Larry, told me that the crane operator left with the mast up. That's against every rule there is. Luckily, we weren't that far up. If the crane had fallen in a different direction, it would have knocked out a big chunk of 10th Street and injured or killed who knows how many people. It was only a one-day headline, thank goodness.

I had some serious lessons to learn about operating a crane. I asked my steel contractor if he knew anyone who owned their own crane independent of the union. (See, if you use your own crane, the union can't stop you.) He said he knew of someone who could help, but he only works in New Jersey.

"Give me his number," I replied.

The next Monday, for the right price, he was on the job with his crane. Well, all hell broke loose. This nonunion operator was moving significant pieces damaged by the accident and some of it was dangerously precarious. Plus, the union didn't like this non-union operator on the site.

Once we had the new crane in place, the union men did not stop taunting the new operator. At times, they would throw coffee at him while he was moving material. I went crazy! Tons of concrete were hanging on the end of the crane mid-air, ten stories up.

I took a video of them in action and went to the police station. They were breaking the law! The union picketers by law had to be a half a block away from the job site. The police boxed them in a pen, and I never had a problem with them again, except once when I was crossing 1st Avenue and one pointed me out and yelled that I was the owner. Then they all started cursing and yelling. I walked directly toward them, and the screaming suddenly stopped.

I said, "Don't blame me. Blame him," pointing to the union guy who had dropped the crane.

The next day, there were only two picketers. The following week, there were none.

Phil tried to come back on the job. He would walk around the workers, threatening to fire them. He even argued with my general contractor, Larry. I didn't know how he even got in. I got into his car with him, trying to defuse the situation, and we drove downtown.

I knew he had not been taking his medication and barred

him from the site again until he got his act together. As we were stopped at a red light, a policeman was crossing right in front of the car. Phil was staring at him. The cop didn't like that and told Phil to get out of the vehicle.

I said to Phil, "Do you want to go to jail again?"

We made peace with the cop and scrammed out of there. Phil drove me back to the site and reluctantly made his way home.

The next day, Larry and I went over to Phil's house to check on him. He was on the stoop in front of his brownstone. I walked over to him and started talking. Halfway through the conversation, Phil suddenly became angry and aggressive.

He started yelling, "You're taping this conversation!"

I remained calm. He may have thought this because I was wearing a cellphone headset, which was uncommon back then. Larry jumped out of his car and got between us to calm things down and then we left.

When I got back to the site, I asked everyone, "How did Phil get in here? If it happens again, you're all off the job."

Larry told his men to lock the doors. He never set foot inside the property again.

To resolve our issues, we met with our lawyers at a restaurant where I was well known. Phil started to lose his cool with me, and I refused to back down. I stared at him harshly and got right in his face. It wasn't that I was so brave and tough. I simply knew that if he even touched me, let alone struck me, I would own him. His bluster would not prevail—he had too much to lose, and we both knew it.

After the unfortunate meeting at the restaurant, the remaining construction work went along without any major bumps. We threw a rooftop party where my friends, co-workers, their wives, and everyone connected to the project came to celebrate this huge milestone. It's kind of amazing standing on the top of a building like this, open on all sides, with the most breathtaking views of the greatest city in the world.

My wife was there and when she got a little too close to the edge one of the workers joked, "Aren't you frightened? We're pretty high up."

She didn't miss a beat. "Are you kidding?" she said, smiling. "I am married to Jerry!"

The original one-story theater building was now seventeen floors below us. We did it and it felt incredible to celebrate it with everyone.

There's a tradition when you top off a building to plant a tree on the roof. Two weeks later while we were on the roof ceremoniously doing so, one of my men pointed out that a plane was flying low and erratically above 5th Avenue. It didn't make sense at all.

Then, the plane hit the World Trade Center.

It was September 11, 2001, and we watched what happened next unfold from that rooftop.

My heart was pounding. At the time, I thought the crash was a freak accident. I didn't see any smoke from the building that had been struck. No smoke, but I saw a hole in the building. The first tower didn't move at all when the plane hit.

It seemed much longer, but it was only about thirty-five minutes before I saw the second plane hit the tower. It came from the direction of Brooklyn across the East River. The plane disappeared between the towers and then a huge fireball came out, the windows blew out, and the fire grew. The smoke was billowing along with the fire.

Now this clearly was an attack, I thought.

One of my steelworkers said to me, pointing at the second building. "That building is going to collapse for sure."

I thought he was crazy—the buildings hadn't moved at all with the crashes.

He then said, "You see that northeast corner exposed by the impact? It's white. It's ash, it's no longer steel. Just watch."

Larry took pictures of everything, awful proof that this was reality and not some Hollywood action movie.

Everything in NYC immediately came to a standstill, including my plans for the rest of the construction. All building material, equipment, and machinery were prohibited below 14th Street.

We tried to support the first responders in any way we could. I brought food for the NYPD, FDNY, and other heroes while my wife offered her psychological services through the Red Cross. She was conducting counseling sessions for hours on end. I also assisted the Red Cross—except I was only on coffee duty. There were a lot of very hard-working people who were very grateful for it though. We took this initiative from 4:00 p.m. until midnight daily for about four months.

After about a month, things in New York started to get back to normal, or as normal as could be after enduring such a powerful blow. New Yorkers are tough. I was petrified that I had lost all my buyers, that no one would even want to be in New York City.

To my surprise, the market bounced back quickly. I had sold

all the lower floors and was able to pay off all construction loans. I kept the penthouse and the floor below for my brother and me. My daughter bought the floor directly below mine.

I started selling units before the building was even finished. When I put scaffolding over the 10th Street entrance, it caught everyone in the neighborhood off guard. The NIMBY types didn't have a chance to organize, and the theater got a lot of flak and was accused of selling out. Everyone thinks they know what's best for others, usually without knowing the full story.

Paula and I went on a much-needed vacation to Italy—something she had scheduled two years earlier. While we were away, I got offers on units and they were selling too fast for us to keep up. It was a good problem. We hadn't even finished the models. I needed to get back to New York immediately.

Business was exploding, and I had to stay on top of things in person. Paula was not thrilled with my distraction. I was working constantly while we were in Italy and ruining what was supposed to be a relaxing vacation together.

I just couldn't help thinking about the job all the time. I even went to a factory to look at a new line of the most magnificent bathroom fixtures. I just had to have them, and I placed an order and had it shipped to me. Italian design is amazing. I can't help myself. I'm always on the lookout for something new and different, no matter where I go.

I knew what was going on. We were setting the market—there were no other comparable buildings nearby. I instructed the brokers to stop selling immediately. When I got back, I increased the sale prices of every unit.

Then I decided to upgrade all the finishes to a higher "uptown" standard. If I had allowed the brokers to sell all the units without putting the brakes on, I would have given at least 30 percent of the value away. I was on point, and I knew it. It was hard to hold on and stay on this train.

I told the head broker that I now wanted to combine the two units on the 15th floor. Each of these units was priced at about $800,000. I made the two into one and raised the price to $2.4 million. She thought I was crazy and asked me sarcastically if I forgot the location of this building. My instincts kicked in, and I knew exactly what I was doing.

We had one showing for the combined unit two days later. The buyer was smitten and said he wanted it, but he had to show it to his partner. When his partner came to visit, he couldn't control himself. "This is fabulous! This is fantastic! I just can't believe it!" I guess they liked it because they offered all cash and didn't negotiate the price. We closed within a week. What was even sweeter was that they didn't want me to finish it—they took it raw. So much for the broker's opinion. That's why I'm the developer, and she's not.

One afternoon, I was at the property, and I got a call from a man who had bought one of the units for his daughter. I had never met either of them at that point. He explained that he and his wife were in the lobby of the building when they overheard the doorman talking about an emotionally challenged tenant. John would keep his window shades wide open for everyone to watch his private escapades. This was apparently intentional, and no one wanted to see any of John's activity. To make it worse, the buyer's daughter had an unpleasant and unfortunate conversation with

John in the elevator. The reason that the father called was to get out of the contract and protect his daughter. He had already put down a 10-percent deposit of $75,000. He knew that there were no legal grounds to break the sales agreement—I could force him to close, or he would lose his substantial deposit.

I was waiting for that one question a man of his intelligence had to ask. I knew it was coming, and then he asked, "Would you let your daughter live in that building?" I took a beat from my acting years and then responded with just two words, "She does." I could see his face turn colors, and I had never even met him. Then there was silence. Everyone knows the next man who speaks loses. I think we broke a record, not one word; it seemed like forever. We must have been disconnected, I thought. He started to stutter, "(Can) I make a suggestion?" I stopped him and said I would let him out of the contract and give him back his deposit. That must have surprised him; he was ready for a fight. For the first time, he was speechless.

I think we impressed each other and became fast friends. He ended up giving me a loan on a property I wanted to develop, and we became partners in other deals. We are the best of friends to this day. So, I'll say it again: keep looking at the puzzle pieces, and you'll find a way to make them fit.

The Theater Building Condos were an absolute success. The theater program never skipped a beat. Our construction gyrations never caused the theaters to go dark, even for one performance. We managed to save the TNC as a haven for creatives, artists, and those who are destined to shine under the bright lights of her lollipop beams.

# The Bowery Hotel (9)

## Paparazzi Catnip

### 2007

Michael Bloomberg is mayor of New York. "The Great Recession" begins and proves to be the longest economic downturn since World War II. Barry Bonds breaks Hank Aaron's home run record of 755. Apple introduces the first iPhone. A relatively unknown senator from Illinois, Barack Obama, declares his candidacy for president. Let's put a shine on the misunderstood Bowery.

"You either get on the train or let it go by." I began this book with this subterranean city metaphor. I feel I have to repeat it every so often. It is a guiding light that shines on my business career as well as the trajectory of my life in general. It won't be the last time you hear me say it. I've always been compelled to follow my intuition, and sometimes I consider it one of my finer strengths.

So here I was going to develop a project on The Bowery, one of the most neglected avenues in the city. It was fraught with all the trappings of a thriller movie: Intrigue. Deception. Cunning and betrayal. Power plays in a court drama and broken friendship that hurt me to the core. It had it all, and it was played by a cast of very interesting characters.

Now, though, The Bowery Hotel—together with the Gemma Restaurant housed at street level there—has become an iconic New York City destination for A-List celebrities, real New Yorkers, and tourists, all in a neighborhood that seemed like the poor, neglected orphan of the city when the story began unfolding.

It all started when I got a call from Max. Max is an attorney and a longtime partner and a friend of mine who conveniently had his office down the hall from me in the medical building. He told me that he had a client who was about to lose a very interesting project without some sort of intervention and that it was "right up my alley." Coming from Max, that sounded quite intriguing, and I was eager to learn more.

Max was a great old-school lawyer who loved to talk in and out of court. He still is. His office was filled with stacks of files everywhere. To me, it seemed cluttered and chaotic, but like a lot of people who use that personal filing system, Max knew where every file was, almost like magic.

To compound the mess, Max had become interested in old watches and timepieces both as a collector and a repairer. This blossomed into a substantial hobby, and Max began furiously buying watches online—hundreds of them. Like the files, they were scattered across his office. Boxes with new purchases arrived every day, it seemed.

Now, when you walked into his office, you'd find Max behind his desk wearing a jeweler's magnifying eyepiece intently puzzling the solution to repairing a watch, even two or three at a time—always with a cigarette dangling out of the corner of his mouth.

When I walked into Max's office to talk about the deal that he thought would be a good fit for me, it was a smoky cloud, as usual. I didn't realize that his client was with him at that moment, and Max introduced me to Frank for the first time.

Frank was built like a box. He could have been a wrestler even; he was so husky and taut. He wouldn't be a guy I'd want to meet in a dark alley somewhere, I thought to myself.

As it was explained to me, Frank had an option on a fifty-year leasehold for a prominent corner on The Bowery and 3rd Street. At that time, he was running a gas station on the property. I was about to hop on another train.

Like all major cities, New York is filled with distinct neighborhoods with a wide spectrum of characteristics and qualities ranging from low to high. When I met Frank, The Bowery was an unusual area of Manhattan and had been for a long time.

Like 5th Avenue, the street itself ran north and south—only nobody would confuse it with 5th Avenue and its assortment of fancy apartments and high-end stores like Saks and F.A.O. Schwartz nestled snugly near the Plaza Hotel. Nope, there were no such comparisons like that to make.

The Bowery—long associated with "skid row"—was a blighted avenue of flophouses and shelters and populated largely by bums, junkies, and street people. It was also the center for lighting and restaurant supplies.

The squeegee men were out in force back then. This was one of the main arteries to Queens. While you were in a car waiting for the light to change, a number of these men would run up and start washing your windows. The drivers were too intimidated not to pay for this unrequested "service."

Just blocks away were entrenched and established homes for families of many cultures living in low, five-story, walk-up tenement buildings. It was the Lower East Side area where immigrants moved in waves when they first arrived in New York. Irish, Jewish, Italian, and Chinese people (among many other nationalities) led these waves of settlement.

The Bowery was near to quite a lot of the best places in Manhattan—Little Italy, SoHo, Chinatown, Greenwich Village. New York University was nearby, too.

There were active transportation hubs that could transport you easily throughout the boroughs. It occurred to me that The Bowery itself had been neglected since the Great Depression with no new development at all for all these years and that I could be a part of its rebirth.

I always felt that I missed out on such an opportunity in the Meatpacking District, and now I had a new chance here, and it could be better than what had happened on the west side of town, I thought. This was going to be my shot to help remake a landmark neighborhood in New York City.

I ended up getting involved with Frank's option despite some stark risks that presented themselves from the very beginning. This included the gas station that Frank was running on the property.

Before we could do anything, we had to make sure that there were no leaks from the gasoline tanks that were buried underground.

The city, state, and federal government were the guard dogs of this environmental issue. If any tanks were found to be leaking, the property would have to be remediated. No one could estimate the scope of that potential problem nor what that cost might be until a shovel went digging. Frank said there was no problem. But what did he know?

I lost a lot of sleep over this project from the moment I signed the deal. I was taking a bigger risk with Frank himself, however. He had no experience, not enough money, and was extremely stubborn at times from the very start of our relationship.

What Frank did have, however, was the option on an exceptionally rare corner property in an undeveloped neighborhood in Manhattan, and I wasn't going to miss this train.

Frank's option called for him to build a 50,000-square-foot building. He had needed someone to join him in the project. For nearly a year, he hadn't found anyone, and his option was about to run out before Max introduced us. It would have been lost forever. I convinced myself that The Bowery made this a rare opportunity, and it was worth the challenges of the partnership that were to come, challenges I anticipated but underestimated.

We structured a deal with me controlling the company until the project was completed. I saved his project; without my involvement, Frank might still be pumping gas. I never expected him to betray me, but that's what ultimately happened. It's a good thing that I kept the upper hand.

Now that I was involved, my experience as a developer kicked in. The real task is to figure out how to build a property that will maximize the allowable usage and create as much profit from each square foot as possible. It's not as easy to do as it may sound, especially in New York City. I immediately noticed that the problem with the original plan was that it didn't generate enough money for all the effort.

I sat down with my long-time architect, Bob Scarano, and planned what we were going to build. I work very well with him; he knows how to interpret my ideas and execute them. Great architects are usually great translators.

Like another project of mine on 10th Street, I added allowable square footage by making the project half a dormitory, which qualified as public space with residential, parking, and retail. Now we had plans for twice the rentable space, which meant paying half the rent and earning twice the income. We were going to build a mixed-use building. With the new concept, there were four revenue streams.

There was a shortage of 20,000 dormitory rooms in New York City at the time. The residential apartments could be spectacular, with magnificent protected 360-degree views.

I envisioned that the penthouses on the fifteenth through seventeenth floors would have unobstructed views of downtown and uptown for miles on all sides. Actually, all the apartments from the fourth floor to the penthouse would have these views of different parts of the city.

Parking was very much in demand in the area, so that would be a winner. The only unknown I saw was the retail space. This would be the first new building on The Bowery since the Great

Depression. There was virtually no foot traffic. I continued to feel viscerally that it would just come, just like it did in the Meatpacking District. (A development with no transportation, and I didn't understand its success.) Only this would be better. I was more convinced than ever.

We broke ground about 2004, and the excavation didn't work quite as planned because of what we found. In the 1920s, the site was the home of a savings and loan company. The building had been demolished, and the property became a gas station. This kept the property on the tax rolls, which I understood was one way of not losing the land to the city.

We found vaults and mazes of hallways to each room. It was like an archeology dig, and this always fascinated me. These passageways were constructed of four-feet by six-feet granite blocks—the very same type of blocks used to build the Brooklyn Bridge. Now you see it in every luxury kitchen in the Hamptons. I didn't have time to repurpose them so I shipped them to my property at Budget Self-Storage, where they remain to this day.

As the project was moving along, I noticed that the men excavating started to work harder than ever. They were looking for some buried treasure, I learned! I spread rumors and coins to keep them moving even faster. I've never seen demolition go so fast.

After adjusting for the stability of the foundation, we began construction. We were using the same construction techniques that I used on our theater building project—lightweight board steel and plank. Everything was going perfectly, moving along very well and quickly. It was really coming together, smooth sailing.

My wife convinced me take a vacation to Ireland. She was the only person who could make me stop working. While we were in Dublin, I got a call in the middle of the night from my general contractor. He told me that we received a stop-work order from the building department. When I asked why, he responded that they said the building is "overbuilt." I told him not to worry and that I'd be there on Monday, and I was.

Monday morning I went to see the commissioner of the building department with my architect, Bob. She was a petite young woman who was very understanding. She said an expeditor had reported that the building was overbuilt and that he had been a constant problem for the department. This expeditor disliked my architect because Bob was getting a lot of jobs in Brooklyn that he wanted, so he tried to create havoc for us spitefully and unnecessarily in every way he could.

It was an unfortunate speed bump, but we resolved the issues with the building department and kept moving along with our project. Every project has its special challenges and set of problems to be solved. This project drove me to the edge.

Bob and I had essentially designed the building together. The most important thing to me was light, view, and air. I also wanted many setbacks (balconies) and a prominent meeting place for dormitory students on the first floor.

After we finished the building plans, I decided to increase the second floor's height from eight feet to fifteen feet to create more options for usable space. When I requested changes like this (and I always did so freely), I made Bob and the structural engineer crazy, but they usually agreed that my ideas were valuable.

Bob knew every trick in the book to get more square feet into a set of plans. It's simple: the more cubic space you give the purchasers, the more creatively they can utilize it and it becomes more valuable to them—and easier to sell.

One day as I walked around the neighborhood, I had an epiphany about our building. It struck me that we were building the gateway to The Bowery. Looking from all directions, it was the focal point. It just instinctively came to me to turn the project into a hotel property instead of a mixed-use building.

The area was becoming perfect for a hotel; I saw it changing. I really thought it would be better than the Meatpacking District. I knew nothing about the hotel business except that this would make a great one.

Frank was initially against it; I had to work hard to convince him. In real estate, most properties are suitable for the purpose they were built but very few can become a real destination location. You know, that's when you get in a cab and say, "Times Square," for example, and the driver doesn't ask for the address. That's the destination location. I wanted that same recognition. Ask any cab driver in NYC to take you to The Bowery Hotel and you'll see we achieved this.

There are so many other factors that help create that type of location that it's almost like alchemy, or magic. It takes an incredible amount of capital to try and buy, design, or build such an icon. Luck, too. This was my epiphany—that we were building a new destination location, not just another hotel.

Making the building a hotel was a great idea except that I had no experience running a hotel. None. We hadn't started work yet on the residences; all we were working on at this stage were the dorms, which were already like hotel rooms. So, I began to look for someone highly skilled in the hotel business that I felt comfortable with. It was critical to my vision to find the right person.

I spent weeks searching for and meeting people, and I didn't find anyone that gave me the confidence I needed to feel in my gut. Some of those I met seemed like sharks and opportunists to me and turned me off. All I wanted was a savvy operator who I could trust.

Many people said, "The Bowery? Are you kidding?"

Perhaps I was wrong, I thought at times. Maybe I should just finish what I started.

Then one night my wife and I had dinner at Balthazar, a great French restaurant in SoHo. They have a banquette in the front with tables where two people sit facing each other. We were seated right next to two men. After a while, I couldn't help but overhear their conversation. They were talking about The Bowery—they were builders. My building came up in the conversation of these random strangers. I couldn't help but break in. I've never been accused of being shy, anyway.

After pleasantries, the hotel came up. I asked if they knew any smart hospitality operators. They said that Harold Keats is the best in the business. I was grateful to get the lead in such an auspicious fashion.

The next day I called Harold and told him what I was doing and what was on my mind. He asked to come meet me and visit the property. When he toured the building, he didn't give any indication of what he felt.

I've certainly seen this nonreaction before and have utilized it often. It's a form of negotiation. Some people call it playing poker. Harold's frozen face and stiff body language showed me that he was a skillful player.

His feelings were exposed when his partner called later that afternoon and said he wanted to come down first thing in the morning. If you have good bait, you catch fish. I knew at once that my hotel idea was spot on.

Harold's partner, Ryan, did the same tour, but unlike Harold, he showed his excitement. He wanted to discuss a deal. He took me to a couple of his hotels. He had many hotels in Manhattan, and I was silently impressed. These were the guys I was looking for. Ryan was selling me. He wanted in.

When we started to negotiate a deal, it became clear that he was more challenging than his initial excitement let on. Negotiations between us began and seemed to go on forever. Ryan said that I just liked to negotiate. The fact was that he wanted what he wanted, and I wasn't going to just roll over. I found giving up control very hard; I had been in control in all my projects until that point.

Early in my career, I learned that when I wasn't in control the projects didn't make money. Ryan projected wealth and was very conservative. I wanted full control over the upper three floors, the fifteenth through seventeenth, and part of the fourteenth, as well. They agreed to the arrangement. If or when we acquired the fee (the land below the hotel), the hotel would convert to a condominium. Frank and I would own those upper floors as part of the deal.

All things being equal, The Bowery Hotel wouldn't exist in its present form if I didn't learn of Harold Keats from the strangers at Balthazar that fateful evening.

The hotel was a home run. It was so successful that it became an icon, as I had hoped. No one truly ever knows how this happens—like when things go viral on social media. In this case it was my partners who were responsible for every aspect of the hotel's success.

Everyone who was anyone in the entire universe of the arts stays at The Bowery Hotel. Fashion. Cinema. Writers. Painters. They all end up here. As soon as we opened, parties went on all night with mega-stars shining. There were always exclusive events like fashion shows, premieres of some form or another, and bands of all types always with their followers in tow.

It was a real hit and still is! It felt like the runaway success that I experienced with the leisure suit all over again. My ego basked in it all, I must admit.

As you enter the building, held by a suit-clad door man, you walk over a red-carpet rug adorned with the iconic Bowery Hotel logo (a man in a red button jacket, top hat, and cane). You're welcomed at the front desk and given a metal key with silky tassels, no generic key cards around here.

We keep things traditional and analogue to give you a feeling that you don't often get anymore. Such as having copies of the daily newspaper artfully displayed for guests. The weather report is printed daily and framed in the elevators.

The lobby is dim and elegant with oversized leather and ornate chairs. As you walk through to the garden patio or classic old-school bar, you're bound to see someone you recognize from the big screen.

The building and the interior look as if they were built a century ago and the hotel's hospitality service is unparalleled. That, I'm sure, vastly contributed to the property magically becoming a destination icon. Every detail has been thought out and well executed.

Really, in the beginning, I did not know if the hotel would be successful, and I always had an exit strategy. There's an ancient Arabic saying that I like. It goes something like this: Trust Allah, but tie up your camel.

The upper floors were my exit. All I really knew is the building's top floors were of great value. I had negotiated my value and exit plans pretty well, I thought. My camel was safe.

I was becoming notorious again as The Bowery became more and more newsworthy. There was a front-page article in the *Observer* whose headline read: "Hey Sheiks! Leisure-Suit Jerry Is Renting Out Bowery Hotel Penthouses – Just $30K a Month!"

I could never shake that the leisure suit blight I created would turn out to be the joke of the fashion industry. Maybe now I would have the last laugh.

We had one restaurant operating but our original plans called for opening two. Gemma got built and the second one never got off the drawing board. I'm not even sure why. As we were creating the hotel, Robert De Niro came by with his manager because he was looking to open another restaurant at that time. They had heard about the hotel, knew the people involved, and thought it would be a good location and a good fit. Besides being a great actor, he has been very successful in the restaurant business.

I walked over toward him. I admit I was a little starstruck. I heard my partner say, "I don't know, we most likely won't have enough space. The hotel will have a restaurant; I'm not sure we will have any more." I thought to myself: he just closed the door on Robert De Niro. How could he do this? De Niro wanted to see the building, so I took him on a tour. He loved it; he also had an interest in a boutique hotel, so our project was particularly interesting to him. We talked about his films. De Niro was a real guy. I wish we had done a project with him.

## The Original Deal

The original deal had been between Frank, Harold, Ryan, and me. Then Ryan brought in two younger men, Jov and Ian, and said unexpectedly that they would also be partners. I wasn't happy, but he said they were his partners in another hotel. I knew the hotel well, and that helped me feel better.

Ryan said, "Trust me, we're all equal partners."

Sirens should have been going off inside my head.

I met Jov and Ian when we signed the partnership. They were restaurateurs and were responsible for the F&B (food and beverage) of the hotel. These two new men also designed the lobby's bars and the second floor where banquets and events are held. They clearly knew what they were doing, and I recognized it.

They designed Gemma to match the era of the hotel's look; they were masters. Hotel guests experience a VIP walk through the kitchen as they are escorted to their tables. It's a fabulous entrée to the whole Bowery Hotel experience and great theater. The entire frontage of the restaurant has windows that open, and we have seating outside on The Bowery.

I had built a curtain wall for the façade of the building, but no one liked it, particularly the local community. They really hated it and publicized that in the newspapers. In response—and for aesthetic reasons—they decided to add brick to the surface and replaced all the windows with floor-to-ceiling windows. It was one of the many smart moves they made. I admit that freely.

The brick-and-windows retrofit did not come without real cost. This increase in cost was one of those items Frank didn't want to pay. We argued. I told him if we were going to have a special hotel, we had to do it. The building turned out great. It looked like it had been there for generations. Everyone loved it. The Bowery Hotel was the first building you saw when you came to The Bowery; it would surely change this neglected area.

I was positive now, but I originally had so many doubts because the location was surrounded by two men's shelters and the Marble Cemetery—one of the oldest cemeteries in the city, built during one of the Yellow Fever epidemics. I had good reason to be nervous in the beginning. Now, however, I had partners with the guts to see that we were making big waves with this project. We were getting noticed.

Here's more about my original partner, Frank. I believe he had been in a family business all his life. I don't think he had ever built this type of building in New York City, or anywhere else, for that matter. He gave me control because he realized that with my experience, I could make it happen. He was down to the wire on losing his option. I didn't know then how close he came. He was there at the construction site daily learning as much as he could and, occasionally, putting in his two cents. This was fine with me. I like input from partners, and he made good suggestions, but I got the final say.

When it then came to building the upper floors, he only had enough money to build one floor. The two other floors would require him to pay for half of a floor. I agreed to lend him the money needed. I did the upper two floors as one single unit per floor. He divided his floor into three units; I told him he was making a mistake. He could have been right. My way was a much bigger risk.

I rented the two floors for $30,000 apiece. He rented his floor for $18,000 total for the three units. Another example of the bigger risk, the bigger reward. I mention this because of what happens next. It's all about the risk and reward.

Frank took what he had learned and started one and then another project. One was on the Lower East Side, and the other was in Brooklyn. He hired my old GC, which was alright with me, but he never asked—that was also alright. I would get calls from these men asking me to get involved because he didn't know what he was doing. I spoke to Frank to see if he needed anything. Not a word. That was all I could do.

Our tenants were billionaires and artists, which added to the image of the hotel. One such artist was a renowned painter, Domingo Zapata. His social circle included many A-list celebrities, which he often brought to The Bowery. During his residency, he was romantically linked to Lindsay Lohan, which brought some drama, interesting attention, and great publicity. She was barred from the hotel after an incident I won't go into. I told Domingo I would arrange for her to get to his floor, but she would have to use the basement entrance.

Domingo hosted plenty of parties including guests like Johnny

Depp, Leonardo DiCaprio, Adrian Brody, and a Sheikh who is purported to be the world's richest man. Domingo also painted some of the most beautiful women in the world—sometimes using their bodies as the canvas, which most notably happened at New York Fashion Week in 2018.

The total opposite side of Domingo was he worked with children for a couple of mayors of NYC running programs in the public schools. He also painted with the Pope on a mission for peace. He took me on one of his visits. We walked into a building; I think it was just outside the Vatican. We entered a small plain room with very bright lights. There was a large entourage with the Pope.

Domingo got the Pope to paint with him. They did it on plexiglass so the Pope's photographer could shoot pictures through the glass; it was a planned event. Each had black paint brushes, the Pope followed Domingo's strokes. I think the finished painting, which was abstract in nature, was auctioned for charity. I spoke to the pontiff on my agenda items, reading and climate. He was a great listener and encourager. The meeting ended with a blessing.

Before Domingo left The Bowery, he painted the elevator doors as a favor to me.

## The Fee Is On The Table

Alan, the owner of the hotel's fee, invited Frank and me to visit him in Las Vegas. I had met Alan originally in New York when the construction was in progress. He was a young man who was in his early forties. He stood over six-feet-six inches tall and weighed possibly 350 pounds. Alan was indeed a large guy. He was very talkative but had a neediness that I couldn't put a finger on until later.

When we arrived in Vegas, Alan met us at the airport. I didn't recognize him. He must have weighed 160 pounds, having lost perhaps half his weight while still carrying what was left on his tall frame. He looked like a skeleton of the man I saw in New York. It hadn't even been a year since our last meeting. I asked if he was all right. He said he felt perfect and explained that he had surgery to install a gastric band around his stomach to lose weight. His weight loss was intentional, he said.

I had heard of this procedure but never met anyone who had it done. We talked about the gastric band. We went to dinner at one of his hangouts. He ate and drank as copiously as he did before.

I pulled him aside and said, "You think you can live as you did before you had the surgery?"

He said he knew he couldn't but was celebrating because we were there. I knew that wasn't the truth. The reason for telling all of this is because he died shortly afterward. I felt so sorry for him; he was simply a lovely young man.

He had had a bit of a hard life. In his case, money couldn't buy self-respect. It was hard for him because I found out his father dominated everything, and he was a hard taskmaster to Alan. Lacking a father's praise or love can destroy a man. Alan tried to overcome this after his father's death. And he was working on it, but the cumulative abuse he received as a child never left him. I knew that Alan loved his children most, and actively planned a future for them different than the one his father had created for him.

Alan was also bright and very creative. He was part of the team that built the glass skywalk overlooking the Grand Canyon. It was an engineering marvel. It is no small feat to create a new landmark. He said fondly one day he wanted to do something together with me. I said any time, but it was not meant to be.

Frank was closer to Alan's family than I, although his first cousin later told me differently. I had not known my architect in New Jersey was his first cousin until after Alan died. I asked him why Alan never said anything. He told me Alan was very private.

Frank had known the family for many years, his gas station was their tenant, and he stayed in touch with Alan's mother after his death. It seems some Las Vegas lawyers controlled the money from the estate. His mother was constantly in need of cash; Frank would give her money and come to me for some. When they had trouble with the estate taxes, Frank rightfully felt it was the right time to buy the fee, which means the land under the hotel, for the benefit of the partners. That would be more than the cost of the fee depending on the price we paid.

So, the game begins. Everyone agreed that we should buy it— it was a real no-brainer. Frank brought the negotiations as far as he could. He gave Ryan the ball because he had the money to act quickly. That's exactly what the deal needed.

We each sat separately with Ryan to discuss the purchase. I reminded him of the condominium, and he said he didn't need to be reminded because you will still have your condo rights. If either Frank or I said no to the buy, that would end the deal. In both those meetings, he said if you don't have the money now, you can buy in later. That's when it all started.

At that point, my brother and I were splitting our assets. It's always tricky with family when money is involved, ours more than most. The negotiations went on for months and at times it turned into a real ordeal. It felt like we were kids again running around the dining room table. It got bad. I didn't think about the purchase of the fee much because I was so preoccupied. I had my original two partners on the case, and I felt confident of Ryan's skills.

I would check in once-in-a-while to learn how things were progressing from Frank. Everything was going well. Then we closed; to this day, I am not sure when that happened. I congratulated Ryan on the job he had done and asked how much I owed him. My brother and I finally had liquidated some assets and continued to negotiate with others.

Unknown to me, the hotel didn't purchase the fee. My partners purchased the fee under another company that didn't include Frank or me. I couldn't understand how this could have happened. Frank was there at the closing. When I asked him point-blank how he stood by and let this happen without telling me, he said there were tax issues. I told him we could have formed a new partnership to deal with the taxes. Frank didn't answer me.

All he could say was, "Don't worry, we will come out okay."

One of the partners Ryan brought in never liked the original deal because of our control of the upper three floors. When the fee came available, this was the way to change that. They felt this way because of the hotel's success. I believed we all benefited from that success.

Jov was from California and very creative. (He was the one who said no to Robert De Niro.) He was tall, with a handsome young face with long hair then that he was constantly pushing out of his face. Anything he touched turned to gold. I really can't say anything bad about him. He wasn't wrong about the value of the upper three floors to the deal.

When we first opened The Bowery, there was a knife fight in front of the hotel that started at one of our neighboring buildings. A reporter asked Jov about the knife fight, and he said, "We want to give our guests the feeling of New York. How cool was that?"

That comment even made the *New York Post*. I didn't think it was cool at the time—I thought it was stupid. But Jov was right about the attention, and he was right about not liking the original deal. The only thing he didn't know is he wouldn't be here without our terms for the condos. That was integral to the agreement.

I originally blamed Jov and Ryan for this partnership dispute, but I was wrong. It was Frank who shot me in the back and himself in the foot. I knew they didn't want to convert the hotel to a condo but they needed Frank to agree. But Frank had a fiduciary responsibility to our company and me.

I had developed a good relationship with Ryan. He did everything he said, and I trusted him above all the other players. Writing this sounds funny, but I still like him. Sometimes after a dispute, you just get over it. You may wonder why after I tell the rest of the story.

I decided to take over the negotiations from Frank about the fee. They acted as if I had done something wrong. This appalled me. Wealthy men always seem to feel they can get whatever they want. I did make a big mistake, though—I trusted Frank.

This wasn't just a misunderstanding between partners; it was grand theft. We had meetings after meetings. In some, we were agreeing, and then we weren't, each pointing fingers at each other for the lack of progress. Finally, Frank, Ryan, and I met with attorneys. We gave them a retainer and set up another meeting with the three of us.

We all went to the lawyers' offices, which seemed to be designed by the same firm that did my MGM offices except they were on the 40th floor overlooking everything (this was a matter of prestige and their fee).

Ryan, as was customary, began the conversation.

He said startlingly, "I don't know why I am here negotiating with tenants who are in arrears."

I responded that we're partners first, and we are up to date on our responsibilities. He said you owe over $100,000 in back rent.

"That's not true," I said. "Call your office."

He did and got a different answer than he expected. Before the meeting, I made sure we had no outstanding invoices. To my surprise, Frank had not paid his portion of the rent for over a year. This was more proof that he was acting in bad faith. That day, I paid for everything so we could go into the meeting with clean hands.

The meeting turned out to be more of a stall. I knew what they were waiting for, the statute of limitations. After some period of time, you cannot sue because you waited too long. You have no case, no matter how right you are. I had asked my attorneys to prepare a complaint to file it at a moment's notice.

Against my attorneys' advice, I sent the complaint to Ryan before I filed the suit. I thought if he saw my total position in black and white, we would come to terms. No one wants a dispute between partners to get out in public. When you file a lawsuit, that's exactly what happens. The press is always waiting for cases they think are newsworthy. I thought our reputations were more important than this issue.

Ryan called and yelled at me on the phone that this was extortion. However, that wasn't my intention, and he didn't understand how much I didn't want to sue. I have to say Ryan was right in his position: if my partner joined him, he didn't have to agree to our condo rights. My attorneys were also right, I gave him too much information. By giving them the suit before it was filed with the court, I gave them a leg up.

When we did file, they were ready and let their money and power try to control the day. Frank initially sat on the sidelines. That's when it became clear he played a much bigger part in the game plan. They couldn't win the case on what I thought were the merits on their own without him. It also showed how much they needed Frank to defend the case.

Let me explain. It seems that Frank was failing in the two projects that he started on his own. On the first, his bank was foreclosing on its construction loan, and the second project had significant structural problems—water damage from leaks. I did not realize just how much trouble Frank was in. I thought there was no need to worry about him because he is the ultimate survivor. What I didn't know was that while he survived, he would bring me down.

What happened at the closing is complete conjecture. Frank said I would not sue (I didn't expect to. I have my father's DNA). Then he said we will be able to work it out. He didn't understand how much money was involved.

I guess Frank was also thinking about the $2 million he had

borrowed from Ryan using his interest in the upper floors and the hotel as collateral (that's everything he had in this project). I knew Ryan had lent Frank some money, but never that much. At first, it was a personal loan to help him out, but the amount grew. That's the only thing that could explain Frank's actions.

You see, first, Frank told me that Ryan would do the right thing. Now he said we should keep the apartments instead of converting them to condominiums as we agreed to do once the fee was purchased. I had a buyer for the three floors for $35 million. Other famous hotels have successfully converted part to a condominium, like the Plaza Hotel. So, there was really no negative effect on the hotel. I may have gotten it all wrong; nothing else makes sense to me. But Ryan believed Frank, and if that were true he would have won this case.

I got some friends and myself to pay off Ryan's loan to Frank and only took the upper floors as collateral, not the hotel (so at least he had something). Then the unthinkable happened. After many warnings, Frank didn't make interest payments on the loan I gave him. I foreclosed on Frank's loan for not making timely payments. You must understand that this was about two years after closing on the fee. I never took his interest in the lease; I just took control of the upper three floors and made all decisions from then on. I never had killer instinct.

Frank initially joined me in the lawsuit against our hotel partners; he even paid his share of the retainer. This turned out to be a very devious act. It gave me confidence that we were a team. He knew all our strategies and in essence, he was their eyes and ears.

By Frank paying a retainer to our lawyers he created a conflict of interest for them. They couldn't represent any action taken against him. That meant I would require another set of attorneys to go after him. Legal representation was all part of their plan. I will explain how much lawyers and the court system played a part in this mess. The lawsuit with Ryan began and once you get to court, the court controls the case.

Now the normal business steps began. Their first salvo was to foreclose on the lease on multiple fronts, which we were ready for. They said we didn't have insurance and were not timely on our rent payments. These charges were empty on the surface.

The following legal tactic was not so easy. I don't think anyone was prepared for this. They sued me with an interpleader, which gave them the ability to hold back all my distributions from the hotel. That action required Frank to tell the court that I had stolen from him.

Suddenly, I realized how dangerous this had become. It was now up to me to defend my reputation. The interpleader was a good tactic, because it took cash flow that may have stopped me in my tracks. But Frank saying anything untruthful about me made me see red. It was a good move, but it wouldn't stand the test of law.

The interpleader case went on for one year before we were even in court. I was still negotiating with Ryan the night before we were due in court. He wanted me to postpone, but I had already postponed a half a dozen times. I said to give me some good faith money and I will. I never heard back. My wife, Paula, who overheard the call, said, "Sue them if he doesn't give you money."

At 10:00 a.m., I was waiting in court with my attorneys Lou Fogel, Craig Kesh, and Richard Williamson. They each had their own skills and together formed a well-rounded and powerful team.

The judge came in about 11:00 a.m. Ryan and Frank were not there; I was the only principal in the court. I'm sure the judge noticed because I was the only person in the whole room who wasn't an attorney. I was not a witness – I was only there to observe.

Most judges have little or no understanding of their cases at the first hearing—all they know is what their clerk tells them. But if the briefs submitted by the attorneys are compelling enough, the judge may read the first few pages. Apparently, this case was convincing enough.

Right out of the gate, the judge knew everything about the subject. First, he ripped Ryan's attorney for bringing the interpleader. Next, he told Frank's attorney he had no standing. If he has a problem with Mr. Rosengarten, he can bring an action. I was already suing Frank in another court.

Then the judge went on. He went after Ryan's attorney, saying he should never have brought this case.

"It has no merit at all. This complaint leaves me cold," he said.

He then continued to chastise and scold their side. "Holding this money is entirely improper," he said.

No one expected him to rule from the bench at the first hearing. That hardly ever happens. My attorneys were quite pleased. Then the other shoe dropped.

The sage among my attorneys asked that I get the distributions, but for technical legal reasons, the judge couldn't release the funds. It took more legal fees and finally one year to get my money released. I did earn legal fees and 9 percent interest on my money.

Now the next hiccup, I had to settle for a lesser amount

because the other side would have appealed, which would have added another year to release the funds. (Our court system favors the rich. And it seems that whoever has the most unscrupulous legal team can draw out a case the longest and usually wins.)

Ryan's attorney was vilified in the press and by other attorneys. When I thought about it later, I realized he was simply going "to the mat" for his client, no matter how wrong it was. I also realized that they could spin their actions any way they wanted. The lawyer didn't care about the notoriety, as long as they spelled his name correctly.

Later Ryan said to me, "You didn't get the money, did you?" I guess at this point, I felt overmatched, but it made me even more determined.

I'm not sure when the depositions took place; this case seemed to be tangled like a weed. It grew wherever it wanted and wouldn't stop until the courts and the attorneys were ready.

Before the depositions, the attorneys prepared me. They told me that nothing you can say at your deposition could win a case; you can only lose at a deposition. Keep your answers short, and don't elaborate on anything extra because it will be used against you.

Ryan had not been given the same advice by his lawyers apparently, he went on-and-on. He even fought with my attorney. (That's why they videotaped the deposition, it's a lot better than looking at the transcript.) Ryan just wasn't prepared for his first lawsuit with a partner, like me. I know Ryan thinks he can control everything, and I guess that's what made him so successful. In this business that is what it takes.

We spent months in discovery. Now the lawyers practiced

their craft. If I recall correctly, they never met a court deadline. The court demanded they fully supply all their information again. They had done a document dump. A document dump means they gave us millions of documents, which even included family pictures, etc. This is a game that lawyers play when they have wealthy clients against poorer ones.

The poorer ones, which was me in this case, will be swamped and crumble. One thing they did include was Ryan's financial statement. Again, it added fuel to my fire. My attorney said they made an error - we never asked for that. I corrected him; they wanted to intimidate me. It showed that I was up against someone with lots more money than me. And Ryan was just one of the group's four heavy hitters I was suing. My attorney had everything documented and were prepared for all the normal tricks of the legal practice.

Now this extremely protracted case went nowhere and ended up in court. Court happens when the person you're negotiating with thinks he holds all the cards. I remember the last time we met at his attorney's office. I was by myself, which is never a good idea when attorneys represent you.

He came out of his attorney's office and asked me "Did you tape conversations with Frank?"

I said, "Of course."

He paused and then asked, "Did you tape me?"

"What do you think?"

He got mad and stomped out of the room. He never got his answer. That was the last time I saw him. He never even came to court after that. This would never settle because they were wrong about the value.

Our day in court was nerve-racking; no one expected this to go on for so long with all the money flowing out. Again, the judge appeared at 11:00 a.m. She was a diminutive woman and spoke with the confidence and strength of someone very much in the proper position. The court was called to order.

Once again, I was the only principal in attendance. I realize that was another tactic to show me they were not concerned. She didn't let anyone speak. She said I've read all the papers. That in itself was great news.

"I'm voiding the defense's answer," she said.

And then she turned her anger towards Ryan's attorney.

I'm not a lawyer, but this was clearly not good for his reputation. He lost his client's case without a trial, and the court reprimanded him. In addition to not liking the games he played in court, she had read the papers and felt going further would be a waste of more taxpayer money. I went to my attorneys to ask what this meant. (I initially thought that this meant we had to go back to the beginning.) They seemed to be shell shocked. They said this was a home run, judges never do this, it was one in a million.

"We won? What does that mean?" I asked.

"We won all the cases," he repeated.

So, there was no trial. The one thing I knew was my case was not a slam dunk because Frank represented me at the closing. Not actually, but legally. This meant it was as if I were there. If this went to trial that would be their defense. If Frank didn't want a condo that would be a nail in my coffin. We had to find out why he did all these things against his own interest and especially mine.

I don't think anyone, including me, realized that we were just getting started on the next leg of the journey. We had to wait for the judge  to write her decision, which would take another three months. After that happened, the other side had the right to appeal. As a matter of fact, they have the right to make two appeals. They ultimately lost both.

Her honor's statement came down. She required an inquest to determine damages; that means the difference in dollars of an apartment verses a condo and the value of the fee. They took both. I could have gone for Specific Performance which meant they would just deliver what was contracted for; but my lawyers said that was a long shot. So, we now had to assemble experts for this inquest. That would suggest just how much money I lost due to their breach.

I knew I couldn't live with myself if I didn't get to the heart of it all. Could I have been so wrong about people? How could I have been so betrayed? I had to see this to the end.

Inquest? I have only heard that word during biblical times. They kept it around just for us. The law uses the term when there is a need to determine damages. This is a whole new case with experts testifying against other experts. I know Ryan didn't think there were any damages.

Now finding the experts is a critical search. I could not know any of these experts as that would disqualify their credibility. The experts are to be impartial, which is understandable since they would testify on my behalf.  My attorneys do the search for the right experts. The only part that I must do is listen to the names and maybe help choose based on their reputation. I never met them till the first day of the inquest.

Ryan was at a disadvantage. He was so well known in real estate that to find someone he didn't know would be a problem. It would be hard for experts to come up with the value because it was a one-of-a-kind property there was nothing to compare it to. We took an excessive amount of time to find the proper experts. We did get the best in the business, and they charged accordingly—even more than the lawyers, which I never even imagined was possible.

I fought with my attorney because I wanted my tenant who tried to buy the condos to testify. Robert wanted to buy all three floors. He had been a tenant for nine years. We used to have breakfast together when I stayed at the hotel. Robert could run any company and have great success, that was just him. He also was smooth, disarming, and smart as a whip.

He had wanted to purchase this property for at least five of those years. I had nothing to sell until we owned the fee. You can't make a condo without owning 100 percent of a property. When there were rumors that we were buying the fee, he made a written offer for $35 million. I couldn't accept the offer until I owned the property. I finally convinced my attorney to have him testify as a witness.

The inquest was assembled in a small room. I think it was the referee's office. Each day there were at least ten people in attendance. I was no longer the only principal—Ryan and Frank were there. The proceedings began with everyone stating their names. Next, a statement was read by the referee explaining the ground rules. One was that the principles would be required to be in attendance every day, and there would be no talking when experts testified.

The first witness was my expert.

"How long have you known Mr. Rosengarten?"

"We just met as we walked into this room."

"You mean you never met him before this inquest?"

"That's correct."

That went on for every one of my witnesses, except my tenant. Now it was their turn to make their opening statement. They said there were zero damages, which my attorney and I expected. From their very first witness, my attorney got them to admit that he or she did work over the years for Ryan. So much for impartiality. Then in a hard-to-believe moment, their crucial witness had listed Ryan as one of her prestigious clients on her website.

As instructed, I testified to the facts. Their attorney started to get into personal points; the referee shut that down right away. Now it was Ryan's time on the hot seat. This was the first time I saw him not control the room. My attorney Lou Fogel frustrated him as well; he reaffirmed the connection with all his witnesses. He got Ryan to admit to writing that the upper three floors were worth $4,000 per square foot, which I still thought was low because of other properties on the market at the time. Unless they sold, the expert couldn't consider them comparable. My floors were more valuable.

When it was my tenant Robert's turn to testify, he spoke with confidence about his willingness to purchase the three floors. He dressed casually, and is a good-looking man and very understated, respectful of the situation. Their attorneys tried to discredit his offer, but he held his ground. The referee directed his first of only two questions during the proceedings.

He asked Robert; "How would you finance the purchase?"

Robert answered, "It was too small a transaction to finance;

I would pay cash."

You could see everyone's face drop, including mine. I never knew how much money Robert had; all I knew was he was my tenant. After the inquest, I found out just how wealthy he really was. The only other question the referee asked was directed to Frank.

"Would you sell to the last witness for $35 million?"

Frank answered incredulously and said, "No."

That was one of the many times he lost all credibility.

The case would be determined on whether Frank and I were considered one entity (a company) or individuals. If the court determined we were combined, they won. If they determined we were each owners, I won. This could have gone either way; a big gamble. Therefore, the condo rights depended on Frank's agreement to convert to condos. The court threw out their answer to the lawsuit and there was no trial. This meant that the court had to determine my damages.

A legal victory doesn't seem to matter. Looking back, it takes too much out of you. I assume both sides feel the same. Ryan's partner Harold may have been right when he said the only one who wins in a lawsuit are the lawyers. It is very rare that a judge throws out a defendant's answer from the bench. It's almost never done. Of course, the other side will take the position that they lost for technical reasons.

This is not true in this case; the judge read the complete case and saw the games the lawyers were playing (badly). And she said this case was a waste of time for the court. She took a real risk, knowing it would be appealed not once but twice. Her reputation was on the line. Her decision was upheld in both forums unanimously.

From the time the fee was purchased, I just couldn't let it go. It started with suspicion and was borne out by facts. I would never knowingly steal from a customer in a restaurant; how could I just lay down for this?

They all thought that I would never sue. I never thought I would. Once I did file the papers, Ryan said that he would take it to the mat. I'm sure it would be an easy win. My father wouldn't sue but my mother would; I don't know what that says about me. It was a never-ending maze. Then the referee came in with a substantial damages amount. The next day, Ryan's attorney called to see if we wanted to settle; this would be the final dance.

## Nobody Wins in a Lawsuit

I had a long time to think about this suit and my partners involved and have come away with some revelations. Since the Nixon years, it's always been said, "follow the money." I've been in this lawsuit for ten years with some very successful men who have good names in business and don't need any more money. Sometimes there are more important things. Like principles and accomplishments. Neither Ryan nor I have been litigious throughout our careers. We all have tried to create value that add to our respective communities. So why did this take place? I have one answer. These are my personal observations only.

There was one person—and only one—who was responsible for this mess. He used both sides against each other and acted as the man caught in the middle.

For the first time in his life, Frank had hit the mother lode of "deep, deep pockets." But he wasn't satisfied with that; he used his leverage and played both of us. As I said, he acted as the wronged party. In the end, he nearly ruined the final settlement.

Ultimately, I will have to live with my other partners. I had a long time to think about this. But, no matter what happens, Frank is a winner. We would get the amount I would have received from the referee's decision. Instead, I settled with Ryan and reduced Frank's gain. Not for my gain but for the other partners who had to pay the award. If I could accomplish that, I would be okay.

I must say something else about Frank. He was put in a world that he wasn't accustomed to. That was not what the original deal was. He did what he thought best to survive. He hurt me financially and wasted a lot of my time. It wasn't right, but it's hard to hold a grudge. That is just not me.

I hope we all turn a new page. I'm satisfied with the settlement. No condos will be at the top of The Bowery Hotel. We will build one of the finest penthouse suites in NYC with over 2,000 square feet of roof area with the best views overlooking the entire city for miles. That was my fallback position from the beginning. It will be a one-of-a-kind destination location in NYC at the top of the iconic Bowery Hotel. I have finished another train ride.

# New Jersey Projects
## Beyoncé for a Day

### 2010

Barack Obama is president while America continues to reel economically from the 2008 financial crisis. The Affordable Health Care Act passes in Congress. The longest solar eclipse of the millennium occurs. Average cost of a gallon of gas in the U.S. is $2.73 and a first-class postage stamp sells for forty-four cents. U.S. begins to dramatically increase number of troops in Afghanistan. SpaceX successfully launches and recovers an unmanned space capsule becoming the first private organization in the world to do so. Justin Bieber—discovered on YouTube in 2008—attracts millions of fans across the world, demonstrating the raw power of social media. So, what's happening in New Jersey while all this is going on?

## Budget Self Storage

One day in 1996 my brother called to say we bought a plastic business. The first thing I said, "What do you mean 'we'?" My next
question was the better one: "Why?" He said it cost nothing, (those
two words don't go together very often) and it comes with two
industrial buildings, one in Newark, New Jersey, and one Passaic,
New Jersey. I hadn't been to New Jersey in years. I had never heard
of Passaic and Newark was where one of the 1967 race riots were.

He said, "I know what you're going to tell me, but let's see if
we can make it work."

That always meant, *here's another project for you*. I didn't get
involved in the plastic business, but when the business closed, I
got another call. This time my brother had an idea, and it was like
the word "plastic" in the movie *The Graduate*. He said, "mini-storage." I don't remember what catastrophe was going on in the
world at this time, but it sounded good to me to go in a different direction.

I said to my brother, "Okay, but you let me have control."

He agreed, but I knew those words weren't worth the air that
came out of his mouth. To his credit, he sat back.

So now, what is mini storage? I knew it from the outside, but
how do you make it a business? The concept is easy: small rooms
for people's junk. I know that's a hard stand to take. But here I
was in Newark, New Jersey. This was an untested area.

So, I took my wife on a tour of the area one Saturday night. I
was amazed to find that we were in a section called Iron Bound.
It was encircled by the railroad tracks, some active. It was populated mainly by hard-working Portuguese. It was like a little

Greenwich Village. We saw a small restaurant packed with customers; it looked like it came from a Portuguese town a hundred years ago.

We couldn't get into the restaurant because they were booked but the host said there was a sister restaurant across the street. The sister was a BIG sister. The restaurant was divided in two. When you went to the right side, it was like walking on the streets of a Portuguese village created by Disney but more authentic.

The bar ran the length of the place. It was packed. We could leave our names and found a place at the bar, not such a small task. I saw things I had never seen before. First, the portions were huge, and waiters would walk around holding a skewer with various meat, such as filet mignon, lamb, and chicken, which they served everyone; it was called Rodizio back in Portugal. It was all you could eat for twelve dollars. This place was my home from then on.

I asked to see the owner and told him what I planned for my building. He was very gracious and said that would work. My wife and I continued to watch the food come out of the kitchen. There was this one chafing dish filled with all types of fish, lobster, crab, and shrimp. They weren't stingy with portions. We ended up taking half of it home and eating leftovers for one week. As I said, this was my place for life. The restaurant is called Iberia, and it's still open to this day.

This project was not my usual, if there is such a thing. But we agreed that the company would have to grow from within. It was the old Breyers Ice Cream building; 90,000-square-feet, four stories with three-foot cork walls. I fitted out an office and hired a company to build fifty storage units. I watched the crew and everything they did. After we rented forty units, we created another fifty ourselves. We did this for a couple of years until we had 900 units, all the space we had in the main building.

There were many sections of the building. One I felt was perfect for a film and music studio. It had a twenty-four-foot-high domed ceiling, and it was 12,000 square feet without any columns. The longest shot a camera could take was 120 feet.

## All of a Sudden, I Grew a Right Hand

Noam was running the storage facility. I'm going to digress to talk about Noam because he had been with me for many years at this point. He was my right-hand man. We first met when he was in his twenties. At that time he was just a young broker starting his real estate career.

All I knew then was that he wanted to sell me a building. I said I was not interested, and he kept coming back. This went on for weeks. He returned so often that I started to get used to him. I'm not sure how it happened, but before I knew it he was my assistant. Little did I know that this headstrong Israeli was to become my second-in-command for many years.

He became even more, like the son I never had. To this day, he's the only person I ever let yell at me—and for that matter, he's the only person who could get under my skin enough that I would yell. When he and I really engaged, the soundproof walls were put to the test. I mean we would scream. I'm not talking about a joke; I mean a serious yelling match. He was worse than my brother and that's saying a lot.

Noam was very persistent, like me. I don't think I had met anyone that became so close to me. And when we had these yelling matches, it was because we disagreed. That was like my legs wanting to go in a different direction than the rest of my body. If we kept score, I think we'd come out even, but it was so painful.

He made his money from deals with no straight salary. We did a lot of projects together. He cut his teeth with The Bowery Hotel; he was my eyes and ears that showed me everything that was wrong. He also rejected a lot of my ideas that worked (those went on my side of the ledger). He was very conservative; I guess that's why we yelled.

Noam was good-looking but would never let you take his picture; he didn't want it to get on the internet. He did a terrific Christopher Walken imitation. We went to a show in the Village called *Everything You Always Wanted to Know About Walken*. The show was made up only of Christopher Walken impersonators. At one point, they asked for volunteers from the audience. He was not going to do anything. So, I put my hand over his head and pointed down. He was coaxed on the stage by audience applause and did his version. I thought it was better than anyone in the cast, and I think so did the audience. Luckily, he didn't get an offer, so he was still my partner.

When we first got to the Breyers' building, I had told my brother it was too big of a building. We couldn't handle it. The building had a ninety-foot by ninety-foot iron sign that deteriorated over the years, spelling the name Byers; it must have gone back to the early 1930s. In any case, it would have cost a fortune to replace it.

One day, I decided to make a fabric sign for Budget Self-Storage to cover it and be an advertisement for our business. You know the type, printed fabric that lets the air go through. I had it made and got my crew to the roof. We all had safety belts. Did you know a safety harness should be worn on your back and not in front? If you wear it in the front and fall, you will break your back. I found that out when I was ninety feet in the air on top of the Breyers sign, and one of my men made me correct mine; at that height, it was more dangerous than wearing it wrong. Add that to your tidbits of random knowledge.

As soon as we tried to raise the fabric, the wind came up, and air did NOT go through the sign as I expected. It lifted my men five feet off the roof. As I watched it happen, I was horrified. I had never put my men in danger like this before (The New Theatre Building was a different kind of fiasco). It was like on a sailboat except, instead of being over water, here they were over a four-story fall to the ground. I shut down the whole operation of hanging the sign.

So, I had to figure out another way of promoting the business. I asked my daughter to design some murals. I guess she did cave in, or just forgot she swore off never working together again. We could put large pictures on the side of the building, which was about 150 feet long. She designed a great logo. These pictures depicted families, some with newborns, families, and singles; they were great.

We explored print ads, too. I put an ad in the Yellow Pages; I noticed all the ads in our sections had no imagination, just photos of storage buildings. I wanted to stand out, so I ran an ad that was a picture of a baby wearing red sunglasses with the tagline, "When that little something needs more room." We started to do business.

There was another building next to the parking lot that could be seen by every car passing on the busy Raymond Boulevard. I decided to put one of the largest American flags in New Jersey on the side. It was about seventy-five feet long. After it was up and running, I put Noam fully in charge. We eventually filled the building with 900 units, and it's still running today.

## Brick Studio

Noam and I had a vision of developing a studio within the Budget building. I still longed for acting, or anything close to it. With the mini-storage profits, we built a music sound studio with three input booths that were totally soundproof. And there was vast space for filming. The first customer originated with my brother. They created a set and shot for over a month.

I realized the business's real potential; we had singing groups using the music section from then on. We even had Sunday morning shows doing interview segments. It became fun for me, all these different artists. I must give Noam total credit for this venture.

One exciting rental was from an acrobatic group that was competing on *America's Got Talent*. They needed the spacious area we could provide. It was like a circus! From arial stunts to amazing gymnastic feats, it was impressive to say the least.

Things had really kicked into high gear. Beyoncé filmed her infamous Pepsi commercial for the Super Bowl at our studio. The airing appeared as if it was entirely live at the halftime of the game but a lot of the footage was pre-recorded at Brick Studio. No one could tell the difference; it all looked live on television and at the stadium. I don't know how they did it. That was our peak.

It took a year to build, and within one day, Hurricane Sandy destroyed the electrical equipment and sound-deadening material. Within hours, all thirty thousand square feet were under eight feet of water. It looked like a rinse cycle. When Howard and I split assets, he got the mini-storage business and what was left of the studio, and he made more storage. It's now run by my brother's son, Fred. It was great while it lasted but the closure of Brick Studio dashed my hopes of ever getting back into acting, my first love.

# Solar Farm
## The War Against Carbon

### 2012

Hurricane Sandy devastates the U.S. East Coast. NYC is particularly hit hard. President Barack Obama is reelected for his second term. Average cost of a gallon of gasoline rises to $3.91. Vladimir Putin is elected president of Russia. Washington state becomes the first district in the modern world to officially legalize the possession of cannabis. The green house creates a stir in Southampton. The energy of doing good.

### A Green Community

When I started to develop my next big project, I was preoccupied with a lot of activity still happening in The Bowery case. It all kept me very busy. Suddenly, I had a new direction and a new enthusiasm that intrigued me as I learned more about the topics unfolding before me. I must give my wife, Paula, credit for this. One day, she came home visibly upset.

I asked her, "Okay, what have I done now?"

Paula flatly told me that not everything revolves around you (this is her favorite line) and then she sadly told me about yellow flags on all the lawns.

"Yellow flags?" I thought.

This was a new one to me. She said the yellow flags were a warning for people and animals not to go on those lawns because they were laced with poisons that would kill the weeds that "ruined" all these beautiful showcase lawns.

Continuing, even more gravely, she went on to say this egotistical practice is destroying the environment while it's poisoning the aquifers that supply us with our precious drinking water. Then, for the first of many times to come, we talked seriously about the environment. All the tidbits of environmental information that I had passively heard over the years woke like a fog passing in my brain.

I could see the urgency Paula felt and her determination to do something. She wrote and designed a flyer describing the perils of the attainment of prize-winning lawns, and she personally delivered them to every house in the neighborhood. I can't say how well the flyers worked and what impact they had, but they marked the small grassroots effort (no pun intended) that was beginning of our focus on environmental stewardship that keeps evolving and growing to this day.

The yellow flags started to attract my attention while driving. I would see them everywhere I went. I decided that I wanted to participate in educating people about the threats of treating the environment poorly, and I thought that I could bring my skills as a real estate developer to promote the cause. I was the inventor of the leisure suit, after all, I laughed to myself, and got millions of people to follow my lead in how they could change their thoughts about how they dressed. Perhaps I could help people change their views on the climate as well. Once again, I was all in and ready to hop on board for a new adventure that, like all train tracks, was sure to have twists and turns.

With my newly found enthusiasm, I started thinking about what I could do. I would build a 100-percent self-sustaining community using the latest technologies and techniques I'd been learning about with my redefined focus. I thought about this on a grand scale because that's me. I am part owner of one hundred acres in Brookhaven, Long Island, New York.

My partners and I have owned this land for over thirty years. The group consists of JL, Kair, Bijon, Alan Kaypor, my brother Howard, and me. This would be the first such community on that scale in the northeast, I believed, and that began to make my entrepreneurial blood flow even more quickly. I was getting completely hooked by the idea of helping to change the world . . . again.

Before I brought this idea to my partners, I decided to build a 100-percent environmentally sound residential home in Southampton so I could learn firsthand exactly what worked—and how best to do it. I always believed that the only way to get people to change their ideas is to lead by example—and not just talk about things. I guess a part of my personality thinks I can show people a new look at something I've created. I would have no problem shaming people into going green if it got results.

This self-sufficient house in the village of Southampton had to be green without giving up any of the luxury and style amenities intrinsic to the eastern end of Long Island. It had to be a showcase, and it had to be extraordinary and within my budget. Building this house would be quite an undertaking because component products would be coming from unestablished companies, often with time delays and not fully tested new products. This project would certainly test my skills.

The style of the house was inspired by a Tuscan villa where Paula and I had vacationed. It was spectacular in its richness and timeliness and was renovated with a very modern interior. That was precisely the style Paula and I wanted to create.

When you walked into the house, you'd be under a ten-foot ceiling. Once you got past the open kitchen, the ceiling of the living room would rise to a wall of glass that lifted up twenty-five feet and opened out with sixteen-foot-wide doors. The entire living room would have a height of thirty-three feet, the width of the entire house. There would be six bedrooms, four on the first level and two on the lower level, and a loft that overlooked everything. Most of my designing, work, and exercise would be done in my office on the loft.

When the green house was finished, I had learned a lot and was itching to build the green community (as sustainable as possible) I envisioned on the hundred-acres. This would be suitable for 300 homes, I thought. First off, we needed a variance since our property was in a commercial zone, and we needed to change that to residential zoning. Before I could start, I had to convince my partners.

The partnership agreement required everyone's approval. This had been the case during the more than forty years we owned the land. During that time, this was the first time we agreed from the start. I sat with my architect, and we planned and designed the project to our satisfaction.

I decided that before I went to the town bureaucracy, I would have to present it to the neighborhood association to see if they would be in favor of this variance. It would be the only project of its kind and scope in the country. If the plan was not approved, I was ready to abandon it and move on to something else. There was always something else to create in my world.

When it came time to make the presentation to the community, it was the first time I had ever met anyone from the area. My lawyer had advised me to stay away from people before the presentation, and that was a mistake, as it turned out. I should have known better.

The presentation was held at a local strip mall that was run-down. I was surprised. It reminded me of the *schul* in the garage I attended as a kid for my religious education. We had our drawings and a model, and I was ready to spread the word about my new vision for the future.

I didn't expect the turnout—there must have been over fifty people. It looked like they had combined a few empty stores for this meeting, and it was disheveled and in need of a good cleaning. There was a stage with a podium ready for me.

As I said, I didn't have a chance to meet any of the people in the audience; they were all strangers. Normally, I like to meet people. It is important for me to get to know them along the way and gain their trust. That's always been my style. There was no chance for that here.

So, I walked right up to the stage, ready to go. My wife, my brother, one of the partners, and my assistant each took a seat, and I began my presentation.

To begin, I said I want to build a residential project that would be an example to the country and change how we use energy. I described the fact that each house would be energy self-sufficient and a marvel of current technology.

Then, before I said the next word, a woman ("Mary") in the third row on the aisle stood up and began to speak, interrupting me. I had no idea who she was, but I was about to find out. It was clear to me that this was her crowd, and it was not my place to take her on as I normally would. I was going to let her continue, and I thought I might lose the group right then.

Then she asked pointedly, "If you want to do what you're talking about, how come you have the property on the market for $15 million?"

I looked at her and said I don't know what you mean. Then I looked at my group for some help, and I saw my brother sink in his seat. I stopped, collecting my thoughts, and while pacing behind the podium looked directly at my brother.

"No, you didn't."

Apparently, he listed the property on Craigslist without my knowledge. Who knows what his intentions were, but it clearly backfired on me. When I realized what had happened, I turned to her.

"I'm not my brother's keeper."

I knew I was dead in the water. I lost all my credibility. She just kept talking like a runaway train.

Then, with a chip on her shoulder, she added, "I'll bet you drive an SUV?"

I sheepishly admitted I did, like I was caught red-handed again, and I took a pause and watched the crowd behind her. They looked at me like she exposed me as a fraud. Again! Then finally I responded that it was a hybrid, and my architect drove a Prius. We walked away with our hats in our hands, and our tails between our legs, as the old sayings go.

I was curious who this woman Mary was because, on the surface, she was just a nondescript, late middle-aged woman. She was plainly dressed and somewhat frumpy in her looks and demeanor.

Mary was a formidable opponent, however. Her knowledge of the law was profound—at least, that's how it sounded. If you can stretch the truth, you can make everything sound profound. It seemed to me that Mary just lived to have control, not unlike others I've run into in my career.

She had a group that she had brainwashed into thinking her goals were just and backed her blindly. I would have respected her more if she even feigned listening to anyone else but herself. So, as it turned out, I would never get the zoning variance, and I would not build my sustainable community. I abandoned the project.

I felt I had to do something environmentally beneficial anyway—I had a statement to make—and I went back to building my green house. When it was finished, I held an open house and printed and distributed a booklet describing all the environmental items in the house.

Many people came, including both builders and buyers. Even

the mayor of the village of Southampton came and cut a ribbon for the opening. I got a very positive reaction, but the entire process didn't do what I wanted and hoped for. I wanted something grander—another leisure suit—a super successful hit that turned a large section of society on their head. That's what drives me in everything I do. It's just who I am.

After removing the community housing project from my plate, things around me began to change. It was 2007, and a major financial crisis was about to hit the country. People were not buying homes, and I didn't sell the green house as I had expected.

My wife and I lived across the street from the completed green house, and I wanted to move into it. I was very pleased with it. Paula emphatically said no—she just didn't wish to leave the home we were living in. It was just the right size for us, and the new house was too big.

It took me five years to win her over but now she loves the house as much as I do. It occurs to me that whenever I design anything, I do it for myself. That is selfish to someone you live with. Over the years, I've been fortunate. Others have liked my ideas and designs, too. If you ask me to describe what I am, I will say I am a designer. I thoroughly enjoy it, and it's the thing I do best, although not necessarily to everyone's taste.


## Solar is the Answer

So, getting back to my thoughts of environmental issues, five years after the community project passed, I was in Italy in a region called Puglia. It's in Southern Italy along the Adriatic coast. It was another one of my wife's trips. If it were up to me, I don't think I would leave Manhattan. However, I have always enjoyed seeing the world with her. It was like when I made trips for textile ideas; I always found something different. It was on this trip to Puglia that I saw my first solar farm. I have come to realize that it was a very significant encounter.

At first, I wasn't sure what it was. I had seen it from the main highway, which was much higher in elevation than the town below and offered a fantastic vantage point. I don't know where we were going, but this was out of our way.

Like many ancient areas, Puglia has narrow streets that wind through irregularly placed stone buildings that were built centuries ago, well before cars came into existence. Our rented SUV was particularly oversized and cumbersome for the area. It was dusk, and we were fortunate that the roads were empty.

Eventually, we saw from the road up above what I initially presumed to be a lake. It was in an industrial area, and on the right, I saw a fence surrounding something I had never seen before. There were hundreds and hundreds of mirrors lying on their side raised about seven feet off the ground. I asked Paula to stay in the car, and I walked over to the locked gate. As I walked, I remembered that Paula was the only one of us who spoke Italian.

An older man walked over to me and started to speak to me in Italian. I waved to Paula in the car to come over, and she did so with her special roll of the eyes for me. She began having an earnest and cordial conversation with the older man. He opened the gate and let us walk around. Then he joined us and told us about what we were seeing.

The Italian people are wonderful. He was sweet and charming to us, these two American strangers. Without even speaking words, he projected a warmth as if we had known each other for years. He told us that the town built what I now know was a solar array installation and that they used all the energy it produced locally.

Walking around the array, I realized that some of the panels were closed underneath with plastic sheets. When we asked about this, he took us under one. We were surprised to see tomatoes, lettuce, string beans, and much more growing heartily in these protected areas. Leave it to the Italians to utilize space so efficiently.

The old man said that the plastic protected against wind and still let in the sun—a perfect place for growing. It made a huge impression on me, and I brought this experience and concept back to the states. It was a long time ago, but it was funny that I once again brought back new and unusual ideas from Europe (same as the fabrics from my past).

I felt like I had a new mission. I took many photos of that startling solar array in Italy and sent them to the other partners of the property in Long Island that had now been lying fallow for nearly forty years. I was going to build a solar farm.

I told my stunned partners in the land that this is the best thing we can do and it's environmentally positive. Plus, I had learned a lot since using solar systems in the green house I built. I certainly overstated my knowledge on the subject a lot, but that never stopped me from doing anything before. I was excited and ready to get on another train.

Sometimes I wonder that if I knew about all the challenges, obstacles, hurdles, and hassles invariably associated with starting a major project, would I still be attracted to it? Like a moth to a flame, it seems to me, and the solar farm project would prove to be no different in its allure.

The first step in any project is to find out how to create it so that it is economically sound. Can it be profitable? I also needed to know if the zoning of the land is such that it can be used "as of right" for this project.

I learned that at the time, there was no existing code for a solar farm in this community—it would become the first privately owned project of its kind in Brookhaven, or even the Northeast. The only solar farm built on Long Island at the time was the publicly operated Brookhaven National Laboratory. They did not have to meet any code or care where the generated energy was dispersed.

It was all so new. When I fully decided that this was good for the public, I decided to go directly to the top decision-makers to start the project on its best foot.

A meeting with the town supervisor was set up. He was very excited about the idea, and he called in his second-in-command to get the lowdown. They were delighted that we were doing this. His assistant said that when we make our presentation to the powers-that-be, the town board, we should go in with two plans. We should show them exactly what we have the legal right to do with our property and then the details of what we propose to do.

After that meeting, I decided to hire a public relations consultant. My partners disagreed. This was the first of many fights—on this one I prevailed. I remembered the meeting with Mary earlier in the process of the green community project and the trouble she stirred. This time I would be prepared, and it was the right move to make.

This is a good time to review the term NIMBY—Not in My Backyard—which includes anyone who wants to object to a project by saying it is terrible for the local public interest. There are First-Amendment laws that protect these people and what they say. They cannot be sued. As I understood it from my lawyer, this protection imbues them with the surety of almost a license to do or say whatever they want with impunity. It's a difficult situation for the subjects of their attention ... like me. That's true for the soundings of government officials as well.

Right from the start, Mary spread disinformation about this project to everyone—neighbors, the press, and government officials. She was a one-person wrecking ball. She cost me millions of dollars. She also cost the environment because her meddling led to the scope of our development changing in a way that delayed actively removing tons of carbon.

She even misrepresented to the neighbors that the solar farm would be ten feet from their property line when she knew full well that the proposed plans called for the farm being located 200-300 feet from their property lines. There was even 800,000 square feet of forest on our land as a buffer.

The town, based on the existing code, made us plant 700 eight-foot-tall trees, even though no one could see the trees through the forest. I told them that the only way to know this farm even existed was from an airplane; 1,000 acres of woodland surrounded it. Once the trees grew, they began to shade our solar panels. They stopped us from pruning them and fined us $25,000. Nothing about this project was easy. I've heard it said that it is the

**Gerald Rosengarten.** Introduction

**Howard Rosengarten—brother.**
Introduction

**John Travolta's iconic Saturday Night Fever look.** Chapter 1

**Brooke Industries Press.**
Chapter 1

**Patchwork denim leisure suit.**
Chapter 1

**Gerald Rosengarten, circa 1970.**
Chapter 1

**Bull from Stand4.** Chapter 4

**The Lift.** Chapter 5

**Slide Watchband prototypes.** Chapter 6

**The Invisible Keypad.** Chapter 6

**Red Square, Moscow, Russia.**
Chapter 7

**New Theatre Building.** Chapter 8

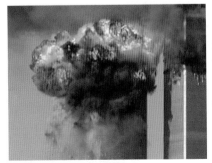

**World Trade Center attack.**
**Photos taken from roof of the**
**New Theatre Building.** Chapter 8

**Bowery Hotel.** Chapter 9

**View from The Bowery penthouse.**
Chapter 9

**Bowery penthouse** Chapter 9.

**Domingo Zapata artwork,
The Bowery Hotel elevators.**
Chapter 9

**Jerry with Pope Francis.**
Chapter 9

**Brick Studio.** Chapter 10

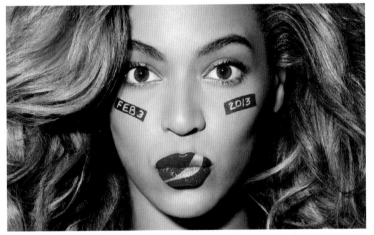

**Brick Studio—Beyoncé Super Bowl commercial.** Chapter 10

**Brick Studio production.** Chapter 10

**Greenhouse.** Chapter 11

**Greenhouse ceiling.** Chapter 11

**Greenhouse bathroom.**
Chapter 11

**Ribbon cutting with Mayor of Southampton.** Chapter 11

**Solar farm.** Chapter 11

**Rendering of aerial view of site.** Chapter 11

5380 Village Road, Long Beach, California 90808    (310) 496-2550, FAX (310) 429-8699

Mr. Jerry Rosengarten, President
A. A. Read, Inc.
88 University Place, 8th Floor
New York, NY 10003

Dear Jerry:

I think it is wonderful that you want to help people improve their reading performance with your kit, *The Rainbow Reader*. Because I am also strongly committed to improving people's performance, I would like to make available to anyone who has purchased *The Rainbow Reader* a $20.00 discount to use personally, for a family member, or for a friend. This $20.00 gift can be used toward further evaluation for the Irlen Filters.

Going beyond the overlays and wearing Irlen Filters can further enhance performance in reading as well as copying, doing math, reading music, using a computer, night driving, and comfort under fluorescent lights.

Just bring your proof of purchase from *The Rainbow Reader* kit to any of the following Irlen Diagnostic Clinics, and this will entitle you to a $20.00 discount towards an individualized color-determining session.

Taking advantage of this opportunity can enhance performance, reduce strain and fatigue, and bring greater success. The enjoyment of reading can be yours long with many other benefits.

Sincerely,

Helen L. Irlen, M.A., M.F.C.C.
Executive Director

**Rainbow Reader.** Chapter 12

first pioneers who catch the arrows. I believe that.

The town and Mary kept making things hard for us. In my world as a real estate developer, it would take about a year, maybe two, to get a permit in New York City to build a seventeen-story building. Here in Brookhaven, the traps were everywhere, and I seemed to fall into each one.

This was uncharted territory for me. Because of the uniqueness of the project, none of the existing codes applied to the solar farm project. They startlingly categorized us as an electric plant, even though a solar farm creates no noise, no emissions whatsoever, no traffic, and in this case, it was out of view, too. Think about just what a traditional electrical generation plant would be in comparison. (And we could have built a conventional project ten feet off the neighboring property, ironically.)

Nonetheless, they made us jump through every hoop imaginable. Our environmental study was a positive deck, and at over 1,000 pages a positive deck is the opposite of what you think—it is the most difficult report of all, as though we were building a city.

Now we were ready with our plans and were prepared to submit them to the board for approval. The supervisor and his assistant came to the hearing. The committee was about to vote, and they asked us to pull our plans because they had come out with a new solar code.

He explained that he wanted our project to be the first solar farm to be approved under the new code. That ended up being a big mistake. It turned out that we went back to square one, and it took another full year to get back in front of the town board.

In the meantime, there were new problems that came up,

primarily that the supervisor now turned against us. Mary had gotten to him and convinced him to go with the local NIMBY groundswell she had created. She wielded her power freely. She created a slogan: *No Green for Green*, which meant don't take down trees for green renewables. This helped turn local people and the press against us.

I was very intuitive initially in hiring my PR consultant at the beginning to counteract the negative shadows being cast around us. One of my partners initially did not like the PR angle because it cost money, but it proved to be a good approach.

The PR guy, Michael Woloz, and I met with every environmental group in the state for months and explained what we were doing. We got most of them to endorse the project. These caring people understood the issues and were beneficial and supportive at all our hearings.

I have always said there are two types of environmentalists: the Preservationist and the Protectionist. The Preservationists have their feet nailed to the ground and dig in to protect the status quo and the environment.

This approach is shortsighted and doesn't consider the future. While we must preserve specific things that affect life, it doesn't answer the need to protect humans and other creatures in the future. It doesn't consider that this is a race and we are losing. Carbon emissions and global warming will destroy our planet. Eventually, if we don't do more to change our behavior and quickly, the race will be lost.

This entire process was very complicated with more layers than an onion. Long Island's utility company is the state-owned and operated Long Island Power Authority (LIPA). Governor Andrew Cuomo, who was the governor at this time, wanted to replace its regular fossil fuel power supply with renewable energy. Even so, I have found that corporate America doesn't want to change, especially because the sun and wind are free and harnessing them would mean that their business may go the way of the horse and buggy. That certainly doesn't make a solar farm look good to them.

In March 2018, the stakes and publicity reached an all-time high. An article appeared in *Newsday* saying that the legislature had passed a law putting two properties in the Pine Barrens, which is protected land that can't be developed. One of those properties was mine, the other was owned by Shoreham. I should explain that if the state takes the property, it gives you construction credits in return, which are basically worthless.

This was a mic-drop moment. I thought it was all over. Then I remembered that it's not law until the governor signs it. My lobbyist had a lot of work to do, but he couldn't assure me that he could get the governor to veto the bill. Howard, who had been on the sidelines, helped. My brother called and got a meeting with the second in command to the governor's commissioner of the environment. The professionals couldn't believe that this happened.

During this tumultuous period, I learned how power really works. I got a flyer by mistake. On it was an invitation honoring "Three Miracle Men." They were the superintendent, a house representative, and a senator. The hostess of the party was none other than Mary. They were celebrating receiving 99 percent approval from the state legislature in less than a month for the Pine Barrens legislation. This was a true feat.

What's funny is I doubt any of those government officials had even read the bill. I know that because I called a dozen or so, and they had no idea what the bill was even about. When I explained it to them, they said they would have never signed that.

Now all my effort was to get to the governor. One of my team members had been in the previous governor's office, and he knew exactly how it works. The governor signs all the bills that are not controversial first and then the rest after that. If he doesn't veto a bill but also doesn't sign it, it proceeds forward and becomes law. So, he had to veto this bill, or we were dead.

We could sue the state, but I never wanted to get into litigation, *especially* against the state. My whole legacy would be the leisure suit and two "David and Goliath" lawsuits. Who would want that?

Everyone on my team was working on Governor Andrew Cuomo. I met his brother, journalist Chris Cuomo, at an Oktoberfest in Southampton. He listened to my problem and asked me to email him. I never heard back. Then one day, without any fanfare, Governor Cuomo vetoed the bill. I was relieved, and I wondered, could anything go wrong now? The answer is, of course it could.

By now, it was getting even worse, and I felt at times as though we would crash and burn. We got a call from the federal Environmental Protection Agency. They said we had to do a study because northern long-eared bats were becoming extinct. Our own expansive ecological report noted that these bats were not in our area, they were not threatened by a loss of habitat, and it was a virus that was damaging the population, but we still had to deal with the EPA straight on.

There was no question in my mind that this was a political maneuver (No Green for Green). They knew that we were short on time. If we lost the power purchase agreements (PPA) with LIPA, we would have no one to sell our energy to and would lose our permit. Due to all this wasted time, we would have lost everything.

Our schedule was to finish the solar farm by the end of that March, and now we had to deal with bats. That gave us one month to clear our hundred acres before the bats started mating. Or we could make wooden boxes open on the bottom and hang them on the trees, like a bat hotel. They wanted us to make 3,000 boxes, which I thought was crazy. So, I arranged to start clearing the property; if I didn't finish in time, I could build the boxes.

Before I cleared the land, Mary got a court order for us to stop work. We in turn went to court and got the stay lifted. You won't believe that as of the writing of this book (four years later) she is still suing us and the town. She really is evil. There is no question she would say or do anything to get her way. I should point out she pays no legal fees. One of her drones is a lawyer and did it pro bono. We, on the other hand, had to pay for all legal shenanigans.

During manufacturing, the framing for the panels was done incorrectly, and no one could prove whose error it was. All the framing had already been erected from the ground, so the panels had to be modified. That's 65,000 solar panels with four connections, each to be modified by hand. That is 260,000 connections reworked.

I repeat, by hand. The weather didn't help. It was a harsh winter. When you're in the construction business, you better be ready for everything.

By the time we finally got the solar farm built, we continued to have unexpected problems. We dealt with LIPA for power purchase agreements and a utility contract. This contract was for them to buy power from us for fifteen years at a specific price. LIPA certainly made it very hard to do business.

For starters, they did not deliver the interconnection to our solar farm to their grid as planned and promised. They were four months late, which meant we didn't have any income for that period, only expenses. Then our bank required us to put up a letter of credit for $700,000, which was not budgeted for. To add insult to injury, LIPA arbitrarily charged us 80 percent more on the interconnection cost than we were quoted. The interconnection cost was to be $4 million, but they billed $7 million. The bank saw this and held all our revenue until this issue was solved.

As of this writing, we have not profited one dollar from this project. LIPA has gone conspicuously silent for two years. I have told my partners that this is good for us because they've made so many blatant mistakes and missteps that they will look foolish in a courtroom. We hired an attorney who said that many utilities don't care about overrun costs. They simply increase the rate they charge the public. We have paperwork on everything when it comes time to present our case.

It all continued. The town stuck its head into the mix. I wasn't sure so I kept looking at my back in the mirror to make sure no one wrote "Schmuck" on it. They gave us a "revised" tax bill for

$1 million yearly. Based on the law, we should have only paid taxes on the land: $89,000. I was too tired of fighting. We settled and got more capacity approved in the deal if LIPA agreed.

I hope to get the right to do a pilot program of growing produce under the panels just like I saw in Italy. New solar panels were developed that produce more energy and are transparent. These panels would be a game-changer for growing food simultaneously with energy production. In this light, we wouldn't have to sell energy to the utility company—we could use it ourselves. We could control the environment under the panels and grow crops twenty-four hours a day with battery storage. And control the temperature to best suit whatever produce we were growing. Some dreams come true when you keep dreaming them.

The solar farm was completed and has been operating since 2018. Public Service Enterprise Group (PSEG) has purchased its output. That means 36,000 to 42,000 tons of carbon has been taken out of the air yearly instead of the mere eighty-four tons of carbon that would have been removed with sixty acres of treed property.

Those numbers, which come from the 2016 report by environmental engineering firm VHB, Vanasse Hangen Brustlin, Inc., bear repeating: 36,000 to 42,000 tons of carbon is akin to taking 6,000 to 8,000 cars off the road.* We should be able to balance between saving trees and reducing carbon.

In any event, the solar farm was a huge learning experience for all parties involved. I hope the lessons learned will benefit the future for everyone. I want to help reshape regulation so that no solar farm

---

\* VHB's Environmental Report can be found at www.jumponthetrainbook.com/resources

will go through what my partners and I did. It took over five years to get a permit and only eight months to build the solar farm. We can save the planet if local government and utilities get out of the way and let science and private enterprise do the job.

I have always tried to make a difference during my career by giving to people by leading by example. Private successes can turn your head, but I've grown to be aware of the greater good, and the future for us and our planet. My new environmental-based goals could help change everything.

All my life, I have really cared about results, whether because of my ego or money. I'm all in now. Stay tuned as I stay focused on the environment. I'll be happy to take off the gloves any time I need to at this point. If it takes me being a whistleblower, that's exactly what I will do.

## Materials and Systems Incorporated into the Green House

Recycled Polystyrene insulation

Recycled road material for roofing

Double roof

Ethanol fireplace for cleaner air

Zero emission windows and doors

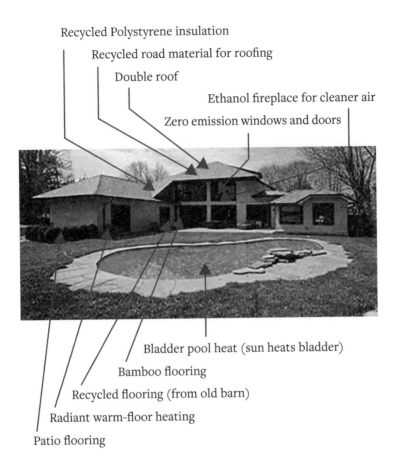

Bladder pool heat (sun heats bladder)

Bamboo flooring

Recycled flooring (from old barn)

Radiant warm-floor heating

Patio flooring

- Solar panels (electricity generation)
- Geothermal (energy-efficient heat)
- Induction cooking (uses less energy)
- Heat pump (creates heating and cooling)
- LED lighting (least costly, long-lasting)

# Rainbow Reader
## It Was Never Your Fault

### 1988-present

World Wide Web is introduced. Astronomers detect the first extrasolar planet. The Soviet Union begins its dissolution. The longest-running Broadway show, *The Phantom of the Opera*, lifts its curtains for the first time. Ronald Reagan is president and Ed Koch is mayor of NYC. All NYC beaches closed after infected syringes and other medical waste washes up on shore. The first WORLD AIDS DAY is observed. Some dyslexics are granted a new solution with a leading-edge technique.

As you read this chapter, you will notice that it's different from the others, and it's the one I believe is the most critical and significant in the book. I am dyslexic and have spent my entire life learning to live successfully with the difficult challenges of reading and learning that are the mark of dyslexic individuals.

I have found a remarkable technique that has helped me profoundly with my own dyslexia, and I wish to spread the word here about it for the benefit of others living with this far-reaching and often debilitating disability. If sharing my personal experiences with dyslexia here helps just one person not fall through the same cracks I've fallen through in my life, it will have served my purpose well.

Some experts say that learning to read is one of the most pivotal and crucial stages in one's emotional development, and in my own case, I agree with this. My dyslexia went undiagnosed for over fifty years.

By definition, dyslexia is a learning disorder that affects the ability to read, spell, write, and speak. This syndrome takes many different forms and can affect each person in various, often insidious ways.

In my case, dyslexia went undetected by my parents and the school system. Unfortunately, diagnosis and treatment remain elusive despite many people struggling with this often-hidden affliction. Kids get hit hard by dyslexia. I know I sure did.

As a child, the tension I felt at school was oppressive—and it got even worse at home at times. I felt under tremendous pressure to please my parents, and I consistently failed, it seemed to me at the time.

I clearly remember being in Mrs. McDonald's fourth-grade class. Sometimes, she would ask us to read to ourselves for what she called an independent reading period. She would roam around the classroom watching us and commenting on how much we progressed in the book.

She never had anything good to say to me, and I could sense that she wasn't happy with my apparent effort. I would be struggling with page one, while my classmates all around me were many pages ahead.

Mrs. McDonald traumatized me. Even though it was over sixty years ago, I can remember her very clearly. She was a heavyset woman, perhaps in her late fifties, and wore dowdy dresses that fit her poorly. I knew she would "catch me" not reading and being near her made me very uneasy. A lot of kids have their own versions of Mrs. McDonald.

One day it was very hot, and the sun baked through the classroom. She asked each student to read out loud. When it was my turn, I got very nervous and began to sweat profusely. I looked around the room and I was just stuck. I had no place to hide. I could barely stand, my legs felt like they were about to buckle. I can feel the unease as though it happened yesterday.

Then I began attempting to read, stammering. The words weren't in order, they came alive in front of my eyes as if they were jumping all over the page. I was standing up there for what seemed like hours when in reality it was just a few minutes.

Hunting clumsily for the next word on the page, I heard Mrs. McDonald say sharply, "Jerry, sit down. Let Johnny show you how it should be done."

I felt like I had just been shot, and every kid in the class burst out in laughter. It was a horrible event for a kid, and I still feel the sting and the shame of my struggles with reading to this day. After this incident, I was placed in remedial classes.

My mother thought constant private tutoring would help, but

it didn't. She was distraught. She would talk to my father constantly about me and she would watch me study every night, just to make sure I really was studying.

I can't tell you how many times I heard:

"He's not trying hard enough."

"He has to put in more time."

"He's lazy, but I know he's smart."

This is certainly how it was—and is—for a lot of kids struggling with undiagnosed dyslexia. Today they have finally understood but they still don't have a real solution.

By learning strategies for hiding my reading disabilities, I somehow got through grammar school. My situation didn't get much better in high school, though. In fact, it worsened. The teachers seemed to want to help me improve my skills, though, and I was able to use that and to learn without reading well.

In hindsight, I recognize that the workaround skills I created to get by—like lobbying for extra time on tests and negotiating for better grades—were blessings. I was granted extra time to practice surviving in this world. I was building and learning to use the tools and skills I would need for the rest of my life. It wasn't easy, or fun, but I made a path for myself. I still do. I found that if you're able to communicate well, you can survive and thrive.

I spent the next fifty years—shamefully at times—keeping all this in the closet. My brother and sister were the only ones other than my parents who really knew just how challenged I was. Like a lot of kids like me, I was constantly ridiculed for being "different." My brother was particularly mean and often cruel. We would fight all the time, but I guess all brothers do at some point.

I did do much better in high school because, as I said, I kept building and refining my communications and other coping skills and was able to simply talk my way through the weeds. My high school teachers were far more forgiving and understanding than Mrs. McDonald, thank goodness.

One teacher made a real impact on me and my interest in school. Mr. DeFalco was a trim man with a full head of jet-black hair. He spoke very smoothly and had a calm and encouraging demeanor. There was something about Mr. DeFalco that made me want to please him. To do so, I worked like I never did before, which meant I was studying constantly.

Other teachers began to recognize my efforts and started to put extra effort into helping me. It made me feel recognized and good about myself. When Mr. DeFalco left teaching to become a lawyer, I was devastated. I have a disdain for most lawyers, and I think that may be in part because of the trauma of Mr. DeFalco leaving teaching to become one.

To my surprise—to everyone's surprise, actually—I started to excel in school and even became more popular. With my new-found confidence, I lost weight and was elected class treasurer. As I was studying more and paying attention to my own strategies for learning, I found that deciphering numbers was a lot easier than unscrambling words and sentences. That fact still comes in quite handy in my business life.

Sometimes, despite my growing adaptation skills, I would find myself in situations where I couldn't hide my reading problems. At home during Passover, everyone in my family was to read a por-tion of the Seder. I studied my part and had it down pat, mostly memorizing it. I was ready to shine.

The book was passed around for everyone to read their parts. My brother's turn came just before mine, and he read his section and then continued through mine. He grinned as he passed me the book for my turn. I couldn't repeat what my brother had just read. So, I stammered my way embarrassingly through the next section in front of my entire extended family.

There have been times during meetings or negotiations where I was asked to read something to myself, and I've had to make excuses, such as that I'd forgotten my glasses. I now have assistants who screen my emails. I have learned to adapt, but it's not been easy.

In May 1988, I was at a cocktail party. In the background, I heard something familiar that caught my ear. It turned out to be a *60 Minutes* segment playing in the other room. A child was speaking, and it sounded like me some thirty-odd years earlier trying to read in front of Mrs. McDonald's class.

I pulled myself away from everyone and watched the show. A man with a full beard, just like mine at the time, was reading from a book. He was struggling to read just like I did. The moderator asked a woman on the show to demonstrate something.

She placed a colored filter on the page, and the bearded man started to read a different section smoothly with good understanding. Then she did the same with a child. It was miraculous. It was unbelievable and I couldn't think of anything else all that day. I didn't sleep at all that night, either.

The next day I was determined to track down the show's producer to find out how to reach this woman with her magical colored reading filters. They kindly directed me to Helen Irlen, founder of the Irlen Institute.

Professor Helen Irlen is a psychologist from California who discovered in the 1980s a method of helping dyslexic kids read by using colored filters laid on top of a page. It wasn't a cure, but it was a sure aid to reading.

For many people, who had problems reading, when they used the filter, they saw the page like it's supposed to be seen. It was astounding. I finally got through to Helen at her offices in California and struck up a conversation after I explained my interest. I was developing the medical building at the time, and I bluntly asked her if she wanted to have offices in Manhattan.

She said yes, and we arranged to get together in New York soon. I told her that I wanted her to test me with her filters when we got together. Two weeks passed, and then she and one of her assistants were in my office. She looked at the potential office space, and we discussed it in detail.

Then she asked if I still wanted to be tested with the filters. Of course, I said yes. She placed many different filters on a printed page. When she put a blue one on the page, I instantly saw the print stop moving for the first time in my life. I could read easily!

To help understand how dyslexia can affect people trying to read (and this can vary from person to person), the print seems to move around the page. Sometimes the words clump in areas so the spacing is nearly impossible to decipher.

In other cases, the white paper overpowers the letters creating difficulty reading for more than a few minutes. Others see "snakes" moving down the page and creating motion and irregular spacing that makes reading nearly impossible.

What's amazing is that a simple five-minute test with a couple of inexpensive filters will correct the problem for many people. What is also amazing is that this remedy is not used in our educational systems.

I want to fix this problem and help kids read, live, and learn better. I don't know how or why these filters work, but it has worked for me for over eighteen years, so I don't need to know how or why.

Helen Irlen discovered that color affects how some people see the printed page. She calls what I described Scotopic Sensitivity Syndrome (SSS), a form of dyslexia that affects 20 percent of learning-disabled children and adults. Color affects how people see print and more.

Different colors work differently for everyone. It's a real phenomenon. I guess it's always been there, but to her credit, Helen discovered it. The world had mostly never heard of her or her institute before the *60 Minutes* segment. She has now been featured on the *BBC*, *National Geographic*, *Good Morning America*, *ABC World News*, and many more, although her methods are still not widely adopted.

Professionals in the field were skeptical and initially weren't interested in performing trial studies. Thousands of people have benefited from the method. I wanted to make it a common test in schools, so I tried. I knew it would change the lives of so many people, particularly the young.

Helen never ended up opening an office in my medical building in New York, so I went to California where she trained me to give tests. I was becoming an evangelist. I tested high school students and even prisoners on Rikers Island. When I tested people who didn't have the condition, all they saw was a colored page and didn't believe the condition existed.

I found the highest sufferers from SSS in prison were Hispanic women. Testing showed that a very high percentage of the prisoner population had SSS. Even getting into Rikers Island was a very startling experience.

Once, after testing one of the inmates, he started crying. I know that if I were in prison and really read for the first time, I would also cry. So many people with dyslexia just fall through the cracks. It makes me question how we teach.

My daughter once told me one of her friends was suicidal because he just couldn't keep up in college, no matter how hard he tried. I spoke to him and sent him the filters, and they worked magically. In fact, he finished at the top of his class. I should explain my opinion about what happens when someone has this problem, which I think will give insight into the high percentage of people with dyslexia who are in prison.

People are divided into two forms of thinking: linear and spatial. Those who are linear are very structured in their thinking and those who are spatial process information more outside of the box. Linear thinkers become lawyers, engineers, and doctors, whereas spatial thinkers become artists, musicians, and inventors. Many people show both traits.

In my day, school learning was presented on a linear basis. Spatial thinkers didn't fit in and became class clowns, troublemakers, or artists. The reason for this is when you can't read and keep up with the rest of the class, you have to find other "out of the box" ways to navigate life. Many spatial thinkers make poor choices along the way and that's why high percentages of incarcerated people are dyslexic, in my opinion.

I told Helen that I wanted to put together a commercial for people to buy the nine-color filters and test themselves. She agreed.

I made the Rainbow Reader kit; it consisted of the filters from Helen's book *Reading by the Colors* and audio cassettes to play while reading. The cassettes were created by my wife, Paula, who is a Doctor of Psychology and employs hypnotism in her work. The first tape had a theme of "It was never your fault," tape two contained background music to read by, and the third tape consisted of background music with subliminal messages of "It's not my fault" incorporated.

With the Rainbow Reader kit finished, I made an infomercial showcasing the filters and cassette sets, which ran at 3:00 a.m. for a month as a test. That was all I could afford to do at the time.

It didn't work. I really had no idea what I was doing as far as creating an infomercial that would get results. I know now that you have to purchase better time slots to air an informercial. The disbelief of the audience that the filters worked was the biggest problem. It still is.

At one point, I saw a small ad in the *New York Post* about a TV show coming to the United States from overseas. They wanted to see new products. I had a couple of other inventions besides the Rainbow Reader, the Invisible Keypad for the first iPhone, and the iStrap for the iPad, but the Rainbow Reader is what I wanted to present to the producers of the show. Maybe this would be a boost to getting the word out, I thought.

When I got to the hotel to make my presentation, there was nobody there. I thought I made a mistake. I asked the doorman of the hotel where the group from London was. He didn't know, but he said they were most likely in the back of the hotel if they were there at all.

I went to the back, but there was only one person standing there alone. I asked if this was the audition for the show from London, and he nodded his head yes. So, I waited. I was determined.

Eventually, they called us in to present our ideas. By this time, two others had shown up and the four of us went in together. There were five long tables with two young interviewers sitting at each one.

I went to the second table and one of the young people asked, "So what do you have to present to us?"

I began my story about the colored overlays and how they solved the reading problem for dyslexic people, and so on. I passed the first test, and they sent me to another table.

There were more direct business questions like:

How many units have you sold?

Do you have a patent?

What business experience do you have?

Right then and there, I thought about how far I had fallen. I was being interviewed by a kid twenty or more years my junior. In any case, I made it to the third round.

That's when I said I wasn't interested in money, that this had a much bigger goal. The show turned out to be *Shark Tank*, which is only interested in commercial products. They summarily bounced me out of there. I had failed again.

I'm going to continue to try and get the filters out there to help people read and live better, easier lives. Interestingly, I once did meet *Shark Tank*'s Mr. Wonderful at The Bowery Hotel's restaurant, Gemma.

I'm still driven by the idea that I can help people experience the wonder of reading. It's not too late.

Since my first use of the filters, numerous studies have proven this is a condition that is solved by color filters. These studies were conducted at Harvard University, Arizona State University, the University of New Orleans, and University of New South Wales in Australia, among others. At least I can prove to my friends that this wasn't another one of my crazy ideas.

Apple has now incorporated "color filters" into their Accessibility settings for Macs, iPhones, and other devices. Other brands most likely do as well. I would recommend being tested by a professional first, but this is a positive step towards more widespread adoption. Once someone affected finds their color, their life is forever changed. You can find more information and get tested at irlen.com.

# Epilogue

A close friend of mine read my manuscript in its early stages and asked me one question. I thought it was worth sharing:

"What lessons have you learned, if any, from writing your book?"

I don't believe I had ever looked at my life in its totality. Everything was divided into segments, with starts, stalls, and finishes, yet they were all interconnected by one common guiding thread: be the first to create something original of value for yourself and others.

My mother gave me strong messages about money, and my father gave me impressions of what goodness is. My parents were children of the Great Depression, and it shaped their views. My father was the archetypal breadwinner and was always fearful of losing hisjob. Fortunately,, that never happened. He was a very religious man and would pray daily. My mother was always talking about wealthy relatives and that my father wasn't earning nearly enough in comparison.

When we grew up, my brother, Howard, wanted deeply to make more money, and I wanted to be hands-on and create. I only knew how to make money from my ideas. Howard was more educated and mechanical in his approach to business, and I was more interested in aesthetics and how things interacted. We were the human equivalents of Microsoft engineering vs. Apple design. We made a good team because of it. He had his law practice and half ownership of the projects, and I owned the other half and had control of 100 percent of our projects.

I've come to the conclusion that both my parents had it right. Their two viewpoints are not mutually exclusive—you can be good and still make money. I hope you recognize that in the book. Some are examples of financial success while also doing good for others. As I'm reflecting, I feel that there's more to do from the giving side of my father's perspective.

Dad, I still have time.

Let's see what the future holds. I have had enough financial successes to support my family and those who helped me along the way.

Now ask yourself: What is enough? When do you help others? The more you have, the more you can help. As a society, we face tremendous disparity in wealth and quality of life. As I look back, I realize I haven't given enough.

Not yet anyway.

I have set my sights on using my resources to help educate others and improve the environment. It's the planet's most significant and most consequential problem. Also, I plan to do more with the Rainbow Reader and help support the mental health needs of others. I hope this book can give me a platform to do even more. I'm no longer just in the background—now, I'm on the inside cover!

I didn't realize the pun, but a platform is a place to speak your mind and also where you go to jump on the train. This book is my platform to speak to a crowd to share my ideas for solutions and become heard.. If you have gotten this far in your reading, you may feel with my experiences that I could have spoken out more for the greater good. Now that's changing. Now is my time to do so.

Saul, Abe, Lenny, and Sal gave me solid and invaluable mentoring in my early years. Even Lester Cohen and Frank taught me an important lesson: you can learn from both the good and the bad—it all just makes you stronger.

Now, start looking for your train. It will come along—wait and pick the right one. Listen to others and learn, but it will always be your decision, your heart's choice. When you find it, jump on and never look back.

Enjoy. It will be a hell of a ride.

# Acknowledgments

Without my wife, Paula, I could never have written this book. She has contributed to each of my projects while always making sure I have a wonderful life. As I had noted earlier, she is a Doctor of Psychology. After reading my story, you can imagine how hard it is for me to live up to her standards. For starters, I never win an argument(!), but she has made me a better person. I can't imagine that it's easy being married to me, but love always wins out. Lucky me.

My daughters, Ilana and Myriah, are two very independent women who never cease to amaze me. They begot our cherished grandchildren Mazzy, Harlow, Nev, and the only boy, Jack. They work full -time and raise their families with their husbands, Mike and Mike. Two Mikes!. Ashley, my niece, and my nephew, Matt, brought Mason and Wes into our lives. I'm known as Poppy to all the grandkids. There's my brother with his wife and their children, Fred and Greg.And, of course, my sister, Caryn, who had two boys and a girl.

I sadly acknowledge and memorialize my brother, Howard; my brother-in-law, Mort; and my nephew, Bryan (they all left far too soon). Bryan departed in his mid-twenties. He was the light in the room, so very full of life. One day he started missing words in his sentences, then an undetected brain aneurysm burst, and we lost him. He remains very vivid in my mind. (I'm sure he's staring down from heaven.) Life would have been empty without all of them. Watching their lives grow and blossom and seeing them deal with their problems yet live heartily brings me great pride and happiness.

One other person I wish to thank is Tessa Lowe. She kept me on track while writing this book, encouraging me each morning on FaceTime and giving me the focus and insight to bring my stories to life. Her bright smile helped me to continue—even when I felt I was wasting my time. She's a jack of all trades and has jumped on the train with my new Apple Watch accessory, the Slide Watchband. Stay tuned!

Special thanks of care go out to Howard and Cindy Lipsky, Kalman and Susan Schmidt, Marty and Kathy Siegel, Bruce and Ellen Belsky, Rabbi Shlomo Uminer, Bhavika Sharma, Prem Siewnarine Hardeo, Elian Warrington, Kathy Ketcham-Wikowitz, Louis Fogel (who helped right a wrong), Max Katz, John Hampton, Alan Kaypor, Bijon Kaypor, Thomas Faltz, Daniel Prokopy, Phil Conserva, Robert Rosenthal, Robert Cohen, Warren Houc, Eric Russo, Marcus Contrervas, Kirt Wilson, Fred Rosengarten, Joe Abraham, Michael Woloz, Robert Scararno, Marc Chiffert, Vicki Kahn, Rick Bogusch, Spencer Haber, Kevin Kotler, Dr. Vivic Garipalli—the first person to read the book's early chapters, and he insisted that I finish it—and his son, Vivic. Paul Shaye and Martin Boxstein were both early readers who encouraged me to continue. Paul was the one who asked the question regarding what lessons

I learned from writing the book.

Howard, my brother . . . one day, he just wasn't there, like he had always been throughout my memories. He was the true love of my life. As two siblings, we lasted together so long, through all the jealousies and fights—right to the very end. Howard and I were like two magnets facing each other. It was difficult to pull us apart, but if you turned us around, no force on earth could put us back together. Ours was the longest relationship in my life. We had many ups and downs but always remained together. My brother was much like my father—he wasn't a real risk-taker. He was the adult in the room, as they say. Howard was my brother by fate, but he also was my best friend by choice. They say blood is thicker than water. Well, blood flows through the heart and that's the strongest part of each of us..

*My relationships are my biggest success of all.*

Me with wife, Paula.

My nephews, Greg (left) and
Fred Rosengarten.

My daughter Myriah (far right)
and her family (from left): Jack,
Mike, and Neve.

My daughter Ilana (back center)
and her family (from left): Mike,
Mazzy, and Harlow.

# About the Author

Gerald Rosengarten is a Brooklyn-born serial entrepreneur whose greatest skill is an extraordinary ability to perceive form and structure–and opportunity–from within disorder, including developing products to deal with dyslexia, reimagining real estate,  and investing early and heavily in solar energy. Rosengarten's life of invention has led to substantial commercial success. His first big hit came in the 1970s with the leisure suit, which became a cultural fashion phenomenon that stoked his confidence and staked his growing desire to build landmark New York projects like the Lofts and the A-list destination, The Bowery Hotel. Today, Rosengarten owns one of the largest private solar farms in the Northeast, located on Long Island's eastern tip, and his creative passions are focused on environmental stewardship and active advocacy for those suffering from learning disabilities.